MOVIE ★ ICONS

DIETRICH

EDITOR
PAUL DUNCAN

TEXT
JAMES URSINI

PHOTOS
THE KOBAL COLLECTION

TASCHEN

HONG KONG KÖLN LONDON LOS ANGELES MADRID PARIS TOKYO

CONTENTS

1

MARLENE DIETRICH: GODDESS

BY JAMES URSINI

DIE GÖTTIN

LA DÉESSE

MARLENE DIETRICH: GODDESS

by James Ursini

Marlene Dietrich once said, "I am not a myth." But by referencing the term, Dietrich only reinforces the fact more emphatically. For, using almost any common dictionary definition of that word, Dietrich *is* a myth.

From 1915 onwards, teenager Marie Magdalene Dietrich utilized the discipline and iron will inherited from her parents to overcome all obstacles and painstakingly create "Marlene Dietrich." Through performances in film, theater, and cabaret, Dietrich crystallized the persona of the bisexual femme fatale. Rooted in the fin-de-siecle obsession with the 'deadly vamp' (seen most remarkably in the works of writers like Charles Baudelaire, Oscar Wilde, and Hanns Heinz Ewers, and painters like Gustav Klimt, Félicien Rops, and Gustave Moreau), Dietrich captivated Berlin audiences with her commanding and haughty manner, often androgynous appearance, and long, languorous legs – all qualities she exploited deep into her senior years.

It is a distortion of the historical record to believe that "La Dietrich" was created by director Josef von Sternberg when he cast the actress in *The Blue Angel*. Dietrich's image as a femme fatale was already fully formed by 1930. Although von Sternberg enhanced the goddess-like allure of Dietrich in the seven films they made together, their work was always a partnership, albeit a stormy and sadomasochistic one, in which the actress trusted her director to project the Dietrich persona through his mastery of the cinematic elements of lighting, costuming, and set design. During this collaboration Dietrich's image evolved from the zaftig, sassy cabaret performer to the sleek, haughty goddess who flirted with both handsome men and beautiful women (a reflection of her own sexual tastes), cuckolded older, dominating men (who often resembled von Sternberg), and always followed her own instincts no matter how potentially destructive the results might be to her or others.

After the couple's personal and professional break-up upon the release of *The Devil Is a Woman* (1935), Dietrich continued to develop her persona without her mentor, expanding the

PORTRAIT (1930)

"I dress for the image. Not for myself, not for the public, not for fashion, not for men."
Marlene Dietrich

types of roles she took as well as humanizing her goddess image. That is not to say Dietrich gave up her aggressive sexuality or superior manner on screen. She simply refined it: in *The Garden of Allah* (1936) she played upon the audience's heartstrings; in *Angel* (1937) she tapped their funny bone; and in *Destry Rides Again* (1939), she combined both elements in the role of a Western femme fatale who takes a bullet for the weak-willed hero.

Dietrich's lifelong disdain for repressive authority, largely rooted in a transgressive independence nurtured during her Weimar years, left her with a visceral antipathy towards all forms of fascism, particularly the Nazi movement. Consequently, during World War Two, Dietrich added yet another dimension to her iconic status by becoming an honorary colonel in the American army and beginning an arduous worldwide entertainment tour of the American frontlines in Europe and North Africa. Young American soldiers, who may have never seen the classic Dietrich films with von Sternberg, reacted to her in much the same way as did audiences from Berlin to Hollywood. They idolized her as she sang sensual songs like 'Lili Marleen' (forever associated with the actress from then on) while decked out in glamorous gowns or joked with them in her trademark sassy manner while always remaining slightly aloof, like a Venus descending into the midst of war.

Disillusioned with the roles offered to her in Hollywood after the war, with the notable exceptions of Billy Wilder's *A Foreign Affair* (1948) and Fritz Lang's *Rancho Notorious* (1952), Dietrich returned to a long-forgotten career, live performance. She toured the world in highly successful one-woman shows. Even as she aged Dietrich continued to project the goddess image on stage, now with a little help from artificial aids. She did return to film for several outstanding performances, most strikingly as Mrs. Bertholt in Stanley Kramer's anti-fascist *Judgment at Nuremberg* (1961). Kramer has acknowledged Dietrich's contribution to the film numerous times in the most grateful and humble terms: "I leaned heavily on Dietrich and her contributions were important. She was a standard-bearer for us. She knew Germany. She understood the implications of the script." Yes, the goddess-femme fatale Dietrich had outlived 'the thousand-year Reich' which had heaped abuse on her for deserting it and working for the enemy. And she had done so in style, a style which has left each new generation firmly in the grip of that defiant young Prussian girl who one morning in 1915 set upon creating an outer image which would not only reflect her inner passions but also live on after its creator's own demise.

MARLENE DIETRICH: DIE GÖTTIN

von James Ursini

Marlene Dietrich sagte einmal: „Ich bin kein Mythos." Mit ihrem Dementi bestärkte sie jedoch die Tatsache umso nachdrücklicher, denn ganz gleich, welches Wörterbuch man auch um eine Definition dieses Begriffs bemüht – die Dietrich *ist* ein Mythos.

Der Teenager Marie Magdalene Dietrich setzte die Disziplin und den eisernen Willen, die ihr die Eltern in die Wiege gelegt hatten, ein, um alle Hindernisse zu überwinden und mit großer Sorgfalt „Marlene Dietrich" zu schaffen. Durch Auftritte in Film, Theater und Varieté kristallisierte Dietrich die Rolle der bisexuellen *Femme fatale* heraus. Ihre Wurzeln gingen zurück auf den „tödlichen Vamp", von dem die Welt des Fin de Siècle besessen war und der sich in seiner eindrucksvollsten Form in den Werken der Schriftsteller Charles Baudelaire, Oscar Wilde und Hanns Heinz Ewers sowie der Maler Gustav Klimt, Félicien Rops und Gustave Moreau manifestierte. So schlug Dietrich das Berliner Publikum mit ihrer hochmütigen und gebieterischen Art in ihren Bann, mit ihrer oft androgynen Erscheinung und ihren langen Beinen – allesamt Qualitäten, die sie bis ins hohe Alter auszunutzen verstand.

Man verkennt die Wahrheit, wenn man glaubt, „die Dietrich" sei eine Erfindung des Regisseurs Josef von Sternberg, der mit ihr die weibliche Hauptrolle in *Der blaue Engel* besetzte. Zu diesem Zeitpunkt hatte Dietrichs Image nämlich bereits eine feste Gestalt angenommen. Obwohl Sternberg in den sieben gemeinsamen Filmen ihren Reiz, der dem einer Göttin glich, noch weiter herausarbeitete, war ihre Arbeit stets eine – wenn auch stürmische und sadomasochistische – Partnerschaft, in der die Schauspielerin dem Regisseur darin vertraute, die Kunstfigur Dietrich durch seine meisterliche Beherrschung der filmischen Elemente Beleuchtung, Kostüm und Ausstattung buchstäblich ins rechte Licht zu rücken. Während dieser Zusammenarbeit entwickelte sich Dietrichs Image von der pummeligen, frechen Varietékünstlerin zur schnittigen, abgehobenen Diva, die sowohl mit gutaussehenden Männern als auch mit schönen Frauen flirtete (ein Abbild ihrer eigenen sexuellen Präferenzen), ältere, dominierende Männer (die oft Sternberg ähnelten) zum Hahnrei machte und stets ihren eigenen Instinkten folgte, ganz gleich, wie zerstörerisch die Folgen für sie selbst oder andere auch sein mochten.

„Ich kleide mich für mein Image. Nicht für mich selbst, nicht für die Öffentlichkeit, nicht für die Mode, nicht für die Männer."
Marlene Dietrich

PORTRAIT (1930)

Nachdem sich das Paar sowohl privat als auch beruflich getrennt hatte und *Der Teufel ist eine Frau* (aka *Die spanische Tänzerin*, 1935) in den Kinos angelaufen war, entwickelte Dietrich ihre Rolle ohne den Mentor weiter, baute ihr Rollenspektrum aus und machte ihr Image etwas menschlicher. Dies bedeutete aber nicht, dass Dietrich ihre aggressive Sexualität oder ihre überhebliche Art auf der Leinwand aufgab. Sie verfeinerte sie lediglich: in *Der Garten Allahs* (1936) drückte sie auf die Tränendrüsen ihrer Zuschauer, in *Engel* (1937) kitzelte sie deren Zwerchfell, und in *Destry reitet wieder* (aka *Der große Bluff*, 1939) verband sie beides in der Rolle einer *Femme fatale* im Wilden Westen, die für den willensschwachen Helden eine Kugel einsteckt.

Weil sie sich in den Jahren der Weimarer Republik eine große persönliche Unabhängigkeit angeeignet hatte, verachtete Dietrich zeit ihres Lebens jede Art autoritärer Unterdrückung und hasste zutiefst alle Formen des Faschismus, insbesondere aber die nationalsozialistische Bewegung. Folglich fügte sie ihrem Status als Ikone während des Zweiten Weltkriegs eine weitere Seite hinzu, indem sie sich zum Ehrenoberst in der US-Armee ernennen ließ und zu einer strapazenreichen Unterhaltungsreise für die amerikanischen Truppen an die europäische und nordafrikanische Front ging. Junge G.I.s, von denen viele niemals einen der Sternberg-Filmklassiker mit Dietrich gesehen hatten, reagierten auf sie ganz ähnlich wie das Publikum von Berlin bis Hollywood. Sie vergötterten sie, wenn sie in ihren traumhaft schönen Gewändern sinnliche Lieder wie „Lili Marleen" hauchte (das fortan häufig mit Dietrich in Verbindung gebracht wurde) und auf ihre typisch freche Art mit ihnen herumalberte, dabei aber stets Distanz wahrte, ganz wie eine Venus, die inmitten des Krieges zu ihnen hinabgestiegen war.

Sieht man von Billy Wilders *Eine auswärtige Affäre* (1948) und Fritz Langs *Engel der Gejagten* (aka *Die Gejagten*, 1952) einmal ab, war Dietrich enttäuscht von den Rollen, die ihr Hollywood nach dem Krieg anbot, und so kehrte sie zu einer längst vergessenen Karriere zurück: den Live-Auftritten. Mit ihrer Ein-Frau-Show reiste sie sehr erfolgreich um die ganze Welt. Selbst jetzt, als sie in die Jahre gekommen war, strahlte Dietrich von der Bühne noch immer das Bild einer Göttin aus, wenngleich sie mittlerweile ein wenig nachgeholfen hatte. Für einige herausragende Rollen kehrte sie noch ein paarmal zum Film zurück. Am eindrucksvollsten war sie dabei als Frau Bertholt in Stanley Kramers *Das Urteil von Nürnberg* (1961), einer Abrechnung mit dem Nationalsozialismus. Kramer würdigte Dietrichs Beitrag zu diesem Film mehrfach mit großer Dankbarkeit und Demut: „Ich habe mich sehr stark auf Dietrich verlassen, und ihre Beiträge waren wichtig. Sie gab uns die Richtung vor, denn sie kannte Deutschland ja. Sie verstand, was das Drehbuch sagen wollte." Ja, Dietrich hatte das „Tausendjährige Reich" jener überlebt, die sie mit schlimmen Verunglimpfungen überschüttet hatten, weil sie ihnen den Rücken gekehrt und für den Feind gearbeitet hatte. Und sie hatte es mit Stil getan – einem Stil, der immer wieder neue Generation in den Bann dieses trotzigen preußischen Mädchens zog, das im Jahre 1915 eines Morgens ausgezogen war, sich ein Image zu schaffen, das nicht nur seine inneren Passionen widerspiegeln, sondern auch noch lange nach dem Ableben seiner Schöpferin lebendig bleiben würde.

MARLENE DIETRICH : LA DÉESSE

James Ursini

Marlene Dietrich a un jour déclaré : « Je ne suis pas un mythe. » Mais en prononçant ce mot, elle n'a fait que renforcer un phénomène déjà existant. Car si l'on s'en réfère à la plupart des définitions courantes du terme, Dietrich est bel et bien un mythe.

Grâce à la discipline et à la volonté de fer héritée de ses parents, Marie Magdalene Dietrich surmonte dès l'adolescence tous les obstacles qui se dressent devant elle pour donner peu à peu naissance à « Marlene Dietrich ». Par ses apparitions au cinéma, au théâtre et dans les cabarets, Dietrich cristallise le personnage de la femme fatale bisexuelle. Puisant dans l'obsession fin de siècle de la « vamp » (particulièrement notable dans les œuvres d'écrivains comme Charles Baudelaire, Oscar Wilde et Hanns Heinz Ewers ou de peintres comme Gustav Klimt, Félicien Rops et Gustave Moreau), Dietrich captive le public berlinois par ses manières hautaines et dominatrices, son allure souvent androgyne et ses longues jambes langoureuses – autant de qualités qu'elle exploitera jusqu'à un âge avancé.

C'est déformer la réalité historique que de croire que « La Dietrich » a été créée par le metteur en scène Josef von Sternberg lors du tournage de *L'Ange bleu*. En 1930, l'actrice a déjà pleinement construit son image. Bien que von Sternberg ait peaufiné son allure de déesse dans les sept films qu'ils ont tournés ensemble, leur œuvre a toujours été le fruit d'une collaboration. Une relation certes houleuse et sadomasochiste, mais dans laquelle l'actrice confie au réalisateur le soin de sublimer son personnage grâce à sa maîtrise des éclairages, des costumes et des décors. Durant leur collaboration, l'image de Dietrich évolue, passant de la chanteuse de cabaret pulpeuse et insolente à la déesse élancée et hautaine. Celle-ci flirte aussi bien avec les beaux garçons qu'avec les jolies filles (reflet de ses propres penchants sexuels), cocufie les hommes mûrs et dominateurs (qui ressemblent souvent à von Sternberg) et suit toujours son propre instinct sans se soucier de l'effet destructeur qu'il peut avoir sur elle et sur autrui.

PORTRAIT

« Je m'habille pour l'image. Pas pour moi, ni pour le public, ni pour la mode, ni pour les hommes. »
Marlene Dietrich

Après leur rupture personnelle et professionnelle à la sortie de *La Femme et le Pantin* (1935), Dietrich continue à développer son personnage sans l'aide de son mentor, élargissant son éventail de rôles tout en humanisant son image. L'actrice ne renonce pas pour autant à afficher une sexualité agressive ou des manières dédaigneuses à l'écran. Elle se contente d'affiner son image. Dans *Le Jardin d'Allah* (1936), elle joue sur la corde sensible du public ; dans *Ange* (1937), elle fait appel à son sens de l'humour ; et dans *Femme ou démon* (1939), elle combine les deux dans le rôle d'une entraîneuse de saloon qui reçoit une balle à la place du héros.

Le dédain que Marlene Dietrich manifeste tout au long de sa vie pour l'autorité et la répression, largement dû à son goût pour l'indépendance et la transgression acquis à l'époque de Weimar, lui confère une antipathie viscérale pour toutes les formes de fascisme, et en particulier pour le mouvement nazi. Au cours de la Seconde Guerre mondiale, l'actrice ajoute par conséquent une nouvelle dimension à son statut d'idole en devenant colonel honoraire de l'armée américaine et en entreprenant une exténuante tournée des fronts européens et nord-africains pour remonter le moral des troupes. Les jeunes soldats américains, dont beaucoup n'ont peut-être jamais vu les classiques de von Sternberg, l'accueillent avec la même idolâtrie que le public international. Qu'elle susurre des chansons langoureuses comme *Lili Marleen* (à laquelle on l'associera désormais) drapée de robes somptueuses ou qu'elle plaisante avec les soldats avec son insolence légendaire, Dietrich conserve toujours un léger détachement, telle une Vénus descendue au milieu des tranchées.

Déçue par les rôles que lui propose Hollywood après la guerre, à l'exception notable de *La Scandaleuse de Berlin* (1948) de Billy Wilder et de *L'Ange des maudits* (1952) de Fritz Lang, Marlene Dietrich fait son retour à la scène, si longtemps délaissée. Son spectacle de chant est acclamé dans le monde entier. Malgré les années, elle continue de projeter sur scène l'image d'une déesse, avec l'aide de quelques artifices. Elle reprendra le chemin des studios pour quelques apparitions remarquées, en particulier dans le rôle de Mme Bertholt dans le film antifasciste de Stanley Kramer, *Jugement à Nuremberg* (1961). Le réalisateur saluera la contribution de l'actrice avec beaucoup de gratitude et d'humilité : « Je me suis largement appuyé sur Dietrich et son apport a été considérable. Elle était notre porte-drapeau. Elle connaissait l'Allemagne. Elle comprenait les implications du scénario. » Oui, Dietrich a survécu au Reich qui l'a traînée dans la boue pour avoir déserté et combattu dans le camp adverse. Elle l'a fait avec élégance, une élégance qui a laissé son empreinte sur les générations à venir. Le monde n'est pas près d'oublier cette jeune Prussienne qui, un matin de 1915, décida de créer une image qui refléterait non seulement ses passions intimes, mais subsisterait long-temps après son propre trépas.

2

VISUAL FILMOGRAPHY

FILMOGRAFIE IN BILDERN
FILMOGRAPHIE EN IMAGES

GERMANY

DEUTSCHLAND

L'ALLEMAGNE

**STILL FROM 'TRAGÖDIE DER LIEBE'
('TRAGEDY OF LOVE', 1923)**
The zaftig Marie Magdalene Dietrich, nicknamed "Leni,"
in one of her early films. / Eine pummelige Marie
Magdalene Dietrich, Spitzname „Leni", in einem ihrer
frühen Filme. / La pulpeuse Marie Magdalene Dietrich,
surnommée « Leni », dans l'un de ses premiers films.

*"Everyone knows how difficult it is to recall the
early years of your life. We all have impressions,
memories that do not always match reality."*
Marlene Dietrich

*„Jeder weiß, wie schwer es ist, sich an die frühen
Jahre seines Lebens zu erinnern. Wir alle haben
Eindrücke, Erinnerungen, die nicht immer mit der
Wirklichkeit übereinstimmen."*
Marlene Dietrich

*« Chacun sait à quel point il est difficile de se
souvenir des premières années de sa vie. Nous
avons tous des impressions, des souvenirs qui ne
correspondent pas toujours à la réalité. »*
Marlene Dietrich

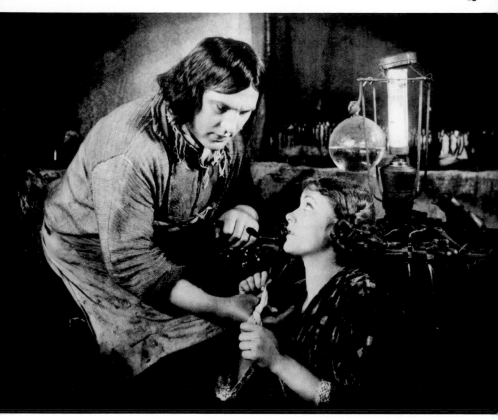

**STILL FROM 'DER MENSCH AM WEGE'
('MAN BY THE WAYSIDE', 1923)**
Dietrich binds the hand of director/actor William
Dieterle. / Dietrich verbindet die Hand von
Schauspieler und Regisseur William Dieterle. / En train
de panser la main de l'acteur/réalisateur William
Dieterle.

**STILL FROM 'DER SPRUNG INS LEBEN'
('LEAP INTO LIFE', 1924)**
A more svelte Marlene pursued by two men, a motif in
many of her movies. / Eine grazilere Marlene, verfolgt
von zwei Männern – ein Motiv in vielen ihrer Filme. /
Une Marlene déjà plus svelte poursuivie par deux
hommes, thème récurrent dans ses films.

STILL FROM 'DER JUXBARON' ('THE BOGUS BARON', 1926)
One of Dietrich's first co-starring roles. / Einer der ersten Filme mit Dietrich in einer tragenden Rolle. / L'un des premiers films dont elle est l'une des vedettes.

"She could easily hold her own. She had the greatest capacity of a person can have; she could laugh at herself."
Fritzi Massary, singer from the Weimar days

„Sie konnte sich gut behaupten. Sie besaß alle Fähigkeiten, die ein Mensch besitzen kann. Sie konnte über sich selbst lachen."
Fritzi Massary, Sängerin aus der Weimarer Zeit

« Elle savait très bien se débrouiller. Elle possédait la plus grande des qualités : elle savait rire d'elle-même. »
Fritzi Massary, chanteuse à l'époque de Weimar

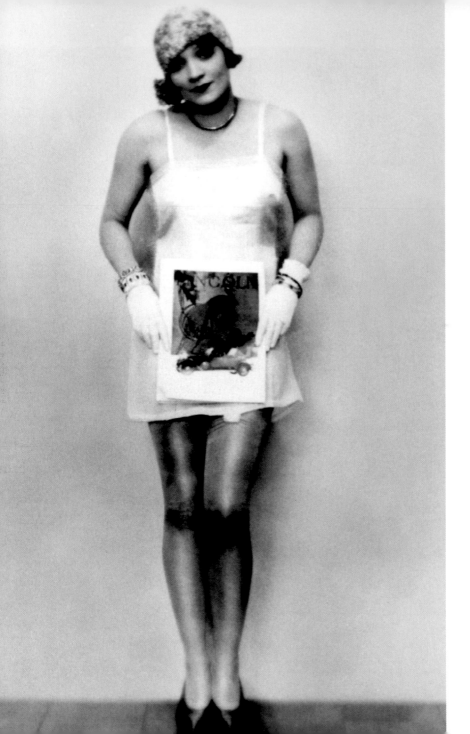

PORTRAIT (1927)
Looking positively domestic (Dietrich loved to cook and entertain) as she signs photographs for fans. / Beim Schreiben von Autogrammen für ihre Fans wirkt Dietrich geradezu häuslich – sie liebte es, zu kochen und ihre Gäste zu bewirten. / Avec ses allures de femme d'intérieur (elle adore cuisiner et recevoir), Dietrich signe des photos pour ses admirateurs.

PORTRAIT (1922)
Lingerie and the birth of a new 'Weimar hot girl.' / Dessous und die Geburt einer neuen „heißen Nummer" in der Weimarer Republik. / Naissance d'une nouvelle « pin-up de Weimar ».

**STILL FROM 'EINE DUBARRY VON HEUTE'
('MADAME DUBARRY', 1927)**
Directed by Alexander Korda, with whom she would
work again ten years later when she was a star. / Unter
der Regie von Alexander Korda, mit dem sie zehn Jahre
später wieder zusammenarbeitete, als sie bereits ein
Star war. / Sous la direction d'Alexander Korda, qu'elle
retrouvera dix ans plus tard, une fois devenue une star.

*"I had no desire to be a film actress, to always play
somebody else, to be always beautiful with
somebody constantly straightening out your every
eyelash. It was always a big bother to me."*
Marlene Dietrich

*„Ich hatte kein Verlangen, Filmschauspielerin zu
werden, immer jemand anderen zu spielen, immer
gut auszusehen und ständig jemanden um sich
zu haben, der einem jedes Lidhaar glattstreicht.
Das ging mir immer auf die Nerven."*
Marlene Dietrich

*« Je n'avais aucune envie d'être actrice de cinéma,
de toujours jouer un rôle, de toujours être belle et
d'avoir constamment quelqu'un en train de me
lisser les cils. Cela m'a toujours ennuyée au plus
haut point. »*
Marlene Dietrich

**STILL FROM 'KOPF HOCH, CHARLY'
('CHIN UP, CHARLY', 1927)**
Prestigious UFA director Willi Wolff directs Dietrich in
this satire of sexual politics. / In dieser Satire auf die
Sexualpolitik spielt Dietrich unter dem angesehenen
UFA-Regisseur Willi Wolff. / Dans une étude de mœurs
satirique dirigée par Willi Wolff, le prestigieux cinéaste
de l'UFA.

STILL FROM 'CAFÉ ELEKTRIC' (1927)
Marlene worked with Viennese matinee idol Willi Forst, with whom she would have an affair. / Marlene arbeitete mit dem Wiener Frauenschwarm Willi Forst zusammen, mit dem sie auch privat eine Affäre hatte. / Son partenaire est l'acteur viennois Willi Forst, idole des femmes avec qui elle aura une aventure.

STILL FROM 'SEIN GRÖSSTER BLUFF' ('HIS BIGGEST BLUFF', 1927)
Marlene (left) displays her lust for diamonds in this jewel-thief caper. / In diesem Film über einen Juwelendieb zeigt Marlene (links) ihre Gier nach Diamanten. / Marlene (à gauche) ne cache pas son goût pour les diamants dans cette histoire de vol de bijoux.

STILL FROM 'PRINZESSIN OLALA' (1928)
The seductress cuckolding the older man, another motif
in Dietrich's oeuvre. / Die Verführerin setzt dem älteren
Mann Hörner auf – ein weiteres Motiv, das sich durch
Dietrichs Werk zieht. / En séductrice cocufiant un
homme plus âgé, autre thème récurrent dans sa
carrière.

**STILL FROM 'GEFAHREN DER BRAUTZEIT'
('DANGERS OF THE ENGAGEMENT PERIOD',
1929)**
By 1929 Dietrich has refined her look and body to fit the
demands of a cabaret/movie goddess. / Im Jahre 1929
hatte Dietrich ihr Erscheinungsbild verfeinert und ihren
Körper auf die Anforderungen an eine Varieté- und
Filmdiva abgestimmt. / En 1929, Dietrich a affiné son
style et sa silhouette pour répondre aux canons des
stars de cabaret et de cinéma.

**STILL FROM 'ICH KÜSSE IHRE HAND,
MADAME' ('I KISS YOUR HAND, MADAME',
1929)**
The Prussian dominatrix side of the Dietrich allure
shines through in this scene. / In dieser Szene
schimmert die preußische Domina durch, die einen Teil
von Dietrichs Reiz ausmachte. / Le côté « dominatrice
prussienne » de Dietrich transparaît dans cette scène.

**STILL FROM 'DIE FRAU, NACH DER MAN SICH
SEHNT' ('THE WOMAN ONE LONGS FOR',
1929)**
Displaying her by-then-famous languorous legs. / Hier
zeigt sie ihre inzwischen berühmten Beine. / L'actrice
exhibe ses jambes déjà célèbres.

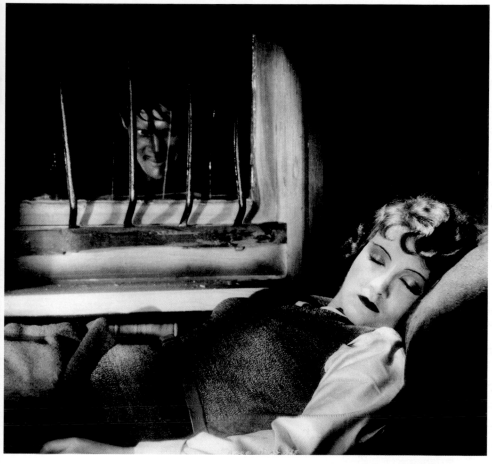

STILL FROM 'DAS SCHIFF DER VERLORENEN MENSCHEN' ('THE SHIP OF LOST SOULS', 1929)
A big-budget UFA production: Dietrich plays an aviatrix who is saved by a ship full of randy men. / Eine UFA-Produktion mit großem Budget: Dietrich spielt eine Fliegerin, die von einem Schiff voll lüsterner Männer gerettet wird. / Dans cette grosse production de l'UFA, elle incarne une aviatrice sauvée par un navire rempli d'hommes lubriques.

PAGE 40
PORTRAIT (1931)
Dietrich meets von Sternberg; the legend is born. / Dietrich trifft Sternberg: die Geburt einer Legende. / La rencontre avec von Sternberg d'où naîtra la légende.

PORTRAIT
The softer side of the goddess. / Die sanftere Seite der Göttin. / Une facette plus tendre de la déesse.

STERNBERG

STERNBERG

STERNBERG

**STILL FROM 'DER BLAUE ENGEL'
('THE BLUE ANGEL', 1930)**
Dietrich and von Sternberg draw on the star's extensive
cabaret background for the nightclub scenes. / Bei den
Szenen im Nachtclub können Dietrich und Sternberg
aus den umfangreichen Varieté-Erfahrungen des Stars
schöpfen. / Pour les scènes de cabaret, ils mettent à
profit son expérience de cet univers.

**PORTRAIT FOR 'DER BLAUE ENGEL'
('THE BLUE ANGEL', 1930)**
Dietrich's Hollywood breakthrough movie and her first
collaboration with lover/director/collaborator Josef von
Sternberg. / Dieser Film, mit dem Dietrich der
Durchbruch in Hollywood gelang, war ihre erste
Zusammenarbeit mit Liebhaber/Regisseur/Mitarbeiter
Josef von Sternberg. / Cette première collaboration
avec le réalisateur Josef von Sternberg, dont elle est la
muse et la maîtresse, lui ouvre les portes de Hollywood.

PAGES 44/45
**STILL FROM 'DER BLAUE ENGEL'
('THE BLUE ANGEL', 1930)**
The director turns the famous Dietrich legs into
cinematic icons. / Der Regisseur verwandelt die
berühmten Dietrich-Beine in Ikonen des Kinos. /
Von Sternberg transforme les célèbres jambes de
Dietrich en mythes cinématographiques.

**STILL FROM 'DER BLAUE ENGEL'
('THE BLUE ANGEL', 1930)**
Emil Jannings initiates the series of humiliated older
men which proliferates in the Dietrich/Sternberg films. /
Emil Jannings bildet den Anfang einer langen Reihe
von gedemütigten älteren Herren in den
Dietrich/Sternberg-Filmen. / Emil Jannings est le
premier d'une série d'hommes mûrs humiliés par la
jeune femme dans les films de von Sternberg.

"Most women set out to try to change a man, and
when they have changed him they do not like him."
Marlene Dietrich

„Die meisten Frauen versuchen, einen Mann zu
verändern, und wenn sie ihn verändert haben,
dann gefällt er ihnen nicht mehr."
Marlene Dietrich

« La plupart des femmes entreprennent de changer
un homme, et quand elles l'ont changé, il ne leur
plaît plus. »
Marlene Dietrich

STILL FROM 'DER BLAUE ENGEL' ('THE BLUE ANGEL', 1930)
Covered in powder Professor "Unrat" enjoys his role as husband/slave. / Völlig eingepudert genießt Professor „Unrat" seine Rolle als Ehemann und Sklave. / Couvert de poudre, le professeur «Unrat» se complaît dans son rôle de mari esclave.

**ON THE SET OF 'DER BLAUE ENGEL'
('THE BLUE ANGEL', 1930)**
Between two men once again, director von Sternberg
and his alter-ego Emil Jannings. / Wieder einmal
zwischen zwei Männern: Regisseur Sternberg und sein
Alter ego Emil Jannings. / À nouveau partagée entre
deux hommes, le cinéaste von Sternberg et son alter
ego Emil Jannings.

*"I was never the ideal [Josef von Sternberg] sought.
He was never quite satisfied. He expected
something we never achieved."*
Marlene Dietrich

*„Ich war nie das Ideal, das Josef von Sternberg
suchte. Er war nie ganz zufrieden. Er erwartete
etwas, das wir nie erreichten."*
Marlene Dietrich

*« Je n'ai jamais été l'idéal que [Josef von Sternberg]
recherchait. Il n'était jamais satisfait. Il tendait vers
un but que nous n'avons jamais atteint. »*
Marlene Dietrich

**ON THE SET OF 'DIE LETZTE KOMPAGNIE'
(1930)**
Dietrich visits Conrad Veidt and director Curtis
Bernhardt on a neighboring UFA set / Dietrich besucht
Conrad Veidt und Regisseur Curtis Bernhardt in einer
benachbarten UFA Kulisse. / Dietrich rend visite à
Conrad Veidt et au réalisateur Curtis Bernhardt sur
un plateau de tournage voisin de l'UFA.

PAGES 50/51
ADVERT FOR 'MOROCCO' (1930)

"MOROCCO"! Hailed as great by Hollywood from the time the first camera started cranking. Brilliant in previews. Chosen by Grauman's Chinese Theatre, Hollywood, from all available product for $1.50 two-a-day glorification. NOW AT ITS FIRST GALA LONG RUN ENGAGEMENT AT THE RIVOLI, NEW YORK, IT SMASHED EVEN BOOM-TIME WEEK-END RECORDS BY OVER $1,000. AND BIGGER BY THE MINUTE! The New York Herald Tribune sums it up: "The cast, the triumph of Marlene Dietrich and the brilliant direction of Josef von Sternberg make 'MOROCCO' a superior picture." It is the type of masterpiece and money-getter that for 18 years has made Paramount PARAMOUNT

GARY COOPER

"Understandably popular, but never so effective and expert as he is in the role of the hero of 'MOROCCO'."
—N. Y. Herald Tribune

ADOLPHE MENJOU

"He is simply grand in 'MOROCCO'. His return is something to write home about." —N. Y. Journal

PARAMOUNT

STILL FROM 'MOROCCO' (1930)
Even macho military men like Tom Brown (Gary Cooper) find Dietrich a force to be reckoned with. / Selbst Militärmachos wie Tom Brown (Gary Cooper) haben es schwer, sich gegen Dietrich zur Wehr zu setzen. / Même un militaire macho comme Tom Brown (Gary Cooper) trouve un adversaire de taille en la personne de Dietrich.

PORTRAIT FOR 'MOROCCO' (1930)
The androgynous Dietrich, created during her Weimar cabaret years and developed with von Sternberg. / Die androgyne Dietrich – eine Schöpfung aus ihrer Weimarer Varietézeit, die Sternberg weiterentwickelte. / Le personnage androgyne de Dietrich, né de ses spectacles de cabaret et peaufiné avec von Sternberg.

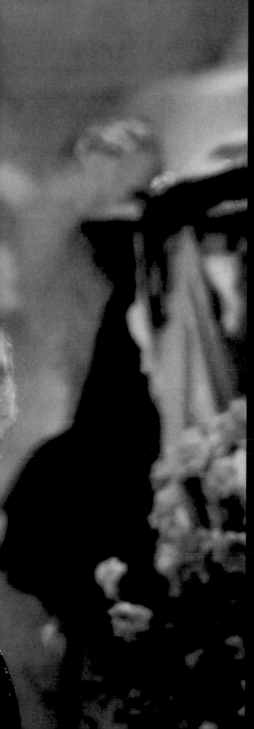

"In America, sex is an obsession, in other parts of
the world it's a fact."
Marlene Dietrich

„In Amerika ist Sex eine Besessenheit, in anderen
Teilen der Welt ist es eine Tatsache."
Marlene Dietrich

«En Amérique, le sexe est une obsession; ailleurs,
c'est un fait.»
Marlene Dietrich

STILL FROM 'MOROCCO' (1930)
Her dress shimmers and her hands grasp him with finely
manicured nails. / Das Kleid funkelt, und ihre Hände
umkrallen ihn mit außerordentlich gepflegten Nägeln. /
Robe scintillante et ongles soigneusement manucurés
pour cette étreinte passionnée.

STILL FROM 'MOROCCO' (1930)
Sternberg's mastery of detail in costuming, lighting, and design served Dietrich's expanding image of herself. / Dass Sternberg jedes Detail in Kostüm, Beleuchtung und Ausstattung im Griff hatte, kam dem weiteren Aufbau ihres Images zugute. / Par sa maîtrise des costumes, des décors et des éclairages, von Sternberg contribue à la construction du mythe Dietrich.

STILL FROM 'MOROCCO' (1930)
The cuckolded older man reappears, this time in the
form of Adolphe Menjou. / Der gehörnte ältere Mann
taucht wieder auf, diesmal in Gestalt von Adolphe
Menjou. / Le mari cocu réapparaît, cette fois sous les
traits d'Adolphe Menjou.

STILL FROM 'MOROCCO' (1930)
When a Dietrich character falls in love, she knows no
limit to her passion, including burning sands. / Wenn
sich eine Figur, die Dietrich spielt, verliebt, ist ihre
Leidenschaft nicht zu bremsen – nicht einmal von
glühendheißem Sand. / Quand l'un de ses personnages
tombe amoureux, rien ne saurait réfréner sa passion,
pas même le sable brûlant.

PAGES 60/61
STILL FROM 'DISHONORED' (1931)
The Rialto decked out to resemble a temple to
Dietrich. / Das Rialto ist wie ein Tempel zu Ehren der
Dietrich geschmückt. / Le Rialto transformé en temple
à la gloire de Dietrich.

PORTRAIT FOR 'MOROCCO' (1930)
A classic Dietrich pose. / Eine klassische Dietrich-
Pose. / Dietrich dans une pose classique.

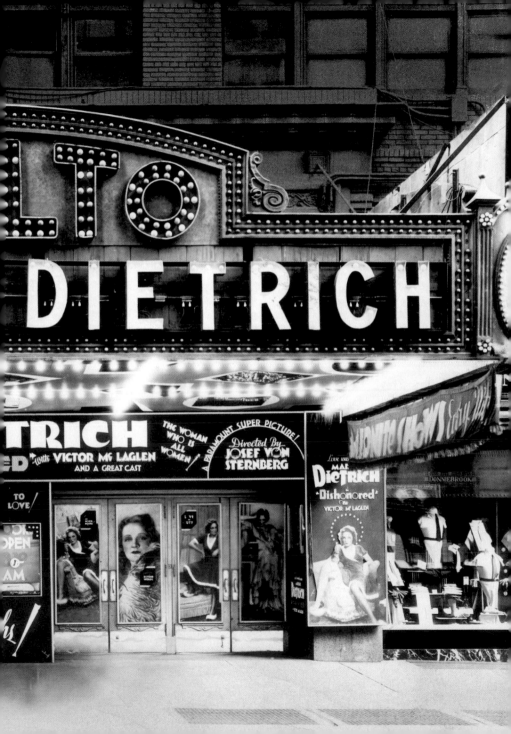

STILL FROM 'DISHONORED' (1931)
Dietrich plays a fictionalized version of the famous
performer/spy Mata Hari. / Dietrich spielt eine
fiktionalisierte Version der berühmten Nackttänzerin
und Spionin Mata Hari. / Dietrich dans une version
romancée de la célèbre danseuse et espionne
Mata Hari.

PORTRAIT FOR 'DISHONORED' (1931)
The fetish side of Dietrich, dressed like a mini-skirted
domme. / Die fetischistische Seite der Dietrich, die hier

STILL FROM 'DISHONORED' (1931)
Another persona for the multi-faceted Dietrich,
the 'naïve' country girl. / Eine weitere Rolle für die
vielseitige Dietrich: das „naive" Mädchen vom Lande. /
Un autre aspect de cette actrice aux multiples facettes :
l'innocente fille de la campagne.

STILL FROM 'DISHONORED' (1931)
Marie/X27 (Dietrich) falls for the brutish Colonel
Kranau (Victor McLaglen). / Marie/X27 (Dietrich)
verliebt sich in den unmenschlichen Obristen Kranau
(Victor McLaglen). / Marie/X27 (Dietrich) s'éprend du
brutal colonel Kranau (Victor McLaglen).

STILL FROM 'DISHONORED' (1931)
In leather, with gun, Dietrich is always the equal to even
the most macho of male stars. / In Leder und mit Pistole
ist Dietrich selbst den machohaftesten männlichen
Stars immer gewachsen. / Vêtue de cuir et armée d'un
revolver, Dietrich traite d'égal à égal les plus machos de
ses partenaires.

PAGES 68/69
ADVERT FOR 'SHANGHAI EXPRESS' (1932)

PORTRAIT FOR 'DISHONORED' (1931)
The intensity of her eyes. / Die Eindringlichkeit ihrer
Augen. / L'intensité de son regard.

MARLENE DIE

Standing Room Again

TRICH

"SHANGHAI EXPRESS"

Directed by

JOSEF von STERNBERG

with

CLIVE BROOK

ANNA MAY WONG, WARNER OLAND, EUGENE PALLETTE

•

DIETRICH! The most popular star on the screen, bar none! In one of the biggest money-makers you've had in a long time. Love! Thrills! Excitement! Dietrich as the fans want her . . . in a new *love-warm* mood! Plus a timely story—leaping from the front pages every day! Plus superb direction of von STERNBERG. Get ready for big dough with Dietrich!

Here IS Box Office!

PARAMOUNT

STILL FROM 'SHANGHAI EXPRESS' (1932)
Shanghai Lily tantalizes yet another military man (Clive Brook) / Shanghai Lily lässt einen weiteren Soldaten (Clive Brook) zappeln. / Shanghai Lily envoûte encore un militaire (Clive Brook).

PORTRAIT FOR 'SHANGHAI EXPRESS' (1932)
Dietrich used costuming as a weapon to conquer the man in the film as well as the spectator in the audience. / Dietrich setzte ihre Kostüme stets als Waffe ein, sowohl um die Männer auf der Leinwand zu erobern als auch das Publikum im Kinosaal. / Dietrich utilise son costume comme une arme pour conquérir son partenaire et ses spectateurs.

"I am credited with Dietrich's discovery. This is not so... I am a teacher who took a beautiful woman, instructed her, presented her carefully, edited her charms, disguised her imperfections and led her to crystallize a pictorial aphrodisiac."
Josef von Sternberg, director

„*Man schreibt mir Dietrichs Entdeckung zu. Dem ist nicht so [...]. Ich bin ein Lehrer, der eine schöne Frau nahm, sie unterrichtete, sie sorgfältig präsentierte, ihre Reize zurechtrückte, ihre Unvollkommenheiten übertünchte und sie dazu brachte, als bildliches Aphrodisiakum Gestalt anzunehmen.*"
Josef von Sternberg, Regisseur

« *On m'attribue la découverte de Dietrich. Il n'en est rien... Je suis un professeur qui a pris une femme superbe, lui a donné des cours, l'a soigneusement présentée, a retouché ses charmes, a masqué ses imperfections et l'a conduite à incarner une sorte d'aphrodisiaque pictural.* »
Josef von Sternberg, cinéaste

PORTRAIT FOR 'SHANGHAI EXPRESS' (1932)
The spiritual Dietrich. / Die vergeistigte Dietrich. /
La part de spiritualité de Marlene Dietrich.

PAGES 74/75
ADVERT FOR 'BLONDE VENUS' (1932)
A working title for 'Blonde Venus.' / Ein Arbeitstitel
(„Tiefe Nacht") für *Blonde Venus*. / Publicité pour
La Blonde Vénus sous un titre provisoire.

Marlene

DIETRICH

DEEP NIGHT

JOSEF VON STERNBERG
PRODUCTION

Dietrich! The most glamorous star of them all! In a story of the world's most glamorous city! The biggest box office role she's ever played! How they'll go for her as the gorgeous stage beauty who takes New York by storm ... the idol of millions and millionaires ... who gives up a brilliant career to marry the man she loves—and sacrifices her soul to save his life! A picture that'll pull 'em straight to your box office. *Play it to the limit!*

PARAMOUNT

STILL FROM 'BLONDE VENUS' (1932)
Dietrich could project the sluttiness of a low-grade
prostitute as expertly as that of a diva. / Dietrich konnte
ebenso gekonnt das Anrüchige einer billigen Nutte
darstellen wie das einer Diva. / Dietrich arbore avec
autant d'aisance l'allure dépravée d'une prostituée de
bas étage que la sophistication d'une diva.

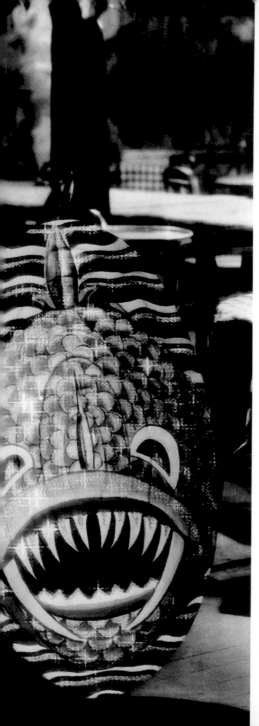

"Darling, the legs aren't so beautiful, I just know what to do with them."
Marlene Dietrich

„Liebling, die Beine sind nicht so schön – ich weiß nur, was man mit ihnen macht."
Marlene Dietrich

« Chéri, ces jambes n'ont rien d'extraordinaire, je sais seulement m'en servir. »
Marlene Dietrich

STILL FROM 'BLONDE VENUS' (1932)
The now-legendary photo of Dietrich in her 'voodoo' costume, stressing the animal side of sexuality. /
Das inzwischen legendäre Foto der Dietrich in ihrem „Voodoo"-Kostüm, das die animalische Seite der Sexualität betont. / La photo désormais légendaire de Dietrich dans son costume « vaudou », qui souligne la dimension animale de sa sexualité.

STILL FROM 'BLONDE VENUS' (1932)
Dietrich bathes contented son Johnny (Dickie Moore)
– she loved playing the 'hausfrau' in her personal life. /
Helen (Dietrich) badet ihren Sohn Johnny (Dickie
Moore) – im Privatleben spielte sie gern die Hausfrau. /
L'actrice, qui donne ici le bain à son fils Johnny (Dickie
Moore), adore jouer à la femme d'intérieur.

STILL FROM 'THE SONG OF SONGS' (1933)
Without von Sternberg, Dietrich continues developing
her various personas. / Ohne Sternberg entwickelt
Dietrich ihre verschiedenen Leinwandcharaktere
weiter. / Loin de von Sternberg, elle continue à
peaufiner ses différents personnages.

PORTRAIT FOR 'THE SONG OF SONGS' (1933)
The goddess laughs. / Die Göttin lacht. / Le rire de la
déesse.

STILL FROM 'THE SONG OF SONGS' (1933)
The Dietrich body in clay, as always pushing the
envelope of Production Code censorship. / Dietrichs
Körper in Ton – wie immer hart an der Grenzen dessen,
was die Selbstzensur der amerikanischen
Produktionsrichtlinien noch durchgehen ließ. / Le corps
de Dietrich sculpté dans l'argile permet de transgresser
les interdits de la censure.

PORTRAIT FOR 'THE SONG OF SONGS' (1933)
Sculptor Richard Waldow (Brian Aherne) finds his
Galatea. / Der Bildhauer Richard Waldow (Brian
Aherne) findet seine Galatea. / Le sculpteur Richard
Waldow (Brian Aherne) trouve sa Galatée.

"So few ever understood my mother's ability to view herself in the third person, a Thing, a Superior Product to be consciously scrutinized for the slightest imperfection."
Maria Riva, Dietrich's daughter

„Ganz wenige verstanden je die Fähigkeit meiner Mutter, sich selbst in der dritten Person zu sehen, als Sache, als überlegenes Produkt, das bewusst auf die leiseste Unvollkommenheit geprüft werden muss."
Maria Riva, Dietrichs Tochter

« Rares sont ceux qui ont compris la capacité de ma mère à se considérer à la troisième personne, comme une Chose, un Produit de qualité supérieure à examiner minutieusement pour y déceler la moindre imperfection. »
Maria Riva, la fille de Marlene Dietrich

PORTRAIT FOR 'THE SONG OF SONGS' (1933)
Wrapped and inviting the viewer. / Eingepackt und einladend für den Zuschauer. / L'actrice emmitouflée nous lance un regard aguicheur.

PAGES 88/89
ADVERT FOR 'THE SCARLET EMPRESS' (1934)

MARLENE DIETRICH

Multi-Ring Circus! A mighty drama. An eye-and-ear spectacle. Thousands of extras, 500 horsemen galloping up Palace stairs in a cavalcade of fury...priests in solemn processional...the most gorgeous wedding ever screened...all against a background of marvelous music and choral singing. **With the Reigning Beauty of the Screen.** MARLENE DIETRICH as the woman of fire, leading Hell-riding Cossacks or as the woman of love, surrounded by her admiring courtiers, has never been more beautiful. Gowned in twenty different costumes, she is truly and incredibly lovely.

THE SCARLET EMPRESS

with John Lodge, Sam Jaffe, Louise Dresser
Directed by JOSEF VON STERNBERG

**ON THE SET OF 'THE SCARLET EMPRESS'
(1934)**
Dietrich's daughter Maria Riva playing the Empress
Catherine as a child, with Dietrich as her hairdresser. /
Dietrichs Tochter Maria Riva spielt Prinzessin Sophie als
Kind, und Dietrich spielt für sie Friseuse. / Marlene
Dietrich recoiffe sa fille Maria, qui incarne l'impératrice
Catherine encore enfant.

**PORTRAIT FOR 'THE SCARLET EMPRESS'
(1934)**
The young Empress Catherine, still innocent. /
Die junge Zarin Katharina, noch voller Unschuld. /
La jeune impératrice Catherine encore innocente.

STILL FROM 'THE SCARLET EMPRESS' (1934)
Captivating Dietrich eyes through veils, a von Sternberg
trademark. / Die betörenden Augen der Dietrich
durch einen Schleier hindurch – ein Markenzeichen
Sternbergs. / Fidèle à lui-même, von Sternberg capte le
regard de sa muse à travers un voile.

**ON THE SET OF 'THE SCARLET EMPRESS'
(1934)**
On the set, Catherine's unhappy marriage to the mad
Emperor Peter. / Während der Dreharbeiten: Katharina
war in ihrer Ehe mit dem wahnsinnigen Zaren Peter
nicht glücklich. / Tournage du mariage malheureux de
Catherine avec Pierre, l'empereur fou.

"I am at heart a gentleman."
Marlene Dietrich

„Im Herzen bin ich ein Gentleman."
Marlene Dietrich

« Au fond, je suis un gentleman. »
Marlene Dietrich

STILL FROM 'THE SCARLET EMPRESS' (1934)
The apotheosis of Dietrich, as Empress, as religious icon. / Dietrich in höchster Vollendung: als Kaiserin und religiöse Ikone. / L'apothéose de Dietrich en impératrice, véritable icône religieuse.

"How do you know love is gone? If you said that you would be there at seven and you get there by nine, and he or she has not called the police yet – it's gone."
Marlene Dietrich

„Wie weiß man, dass eine Liebe erloschen ist? Wenn du gesagt hast, du kämest um sieben, und du kommst erst um neun und er bis dahin noch nicht die Polizei gerufen hat – dann ist sie dahin."
Marlene Dietrich

«Comment sait-on que l'amour est mort ? Si vous dites que vous serez là à sept heures, que vous arrivez à neuf heures et que l'autre n'a pas encore appelé la police, c'est que c'est terminé.»
Marlene Dietrich

**PORTRAIT FOR 'THE DEVIL IS A WOMAN'
(1935)**
Dietrich as Concha, the femme fatale of decadent novelist Pierre Louÿs. / Dietrich als Concha, die berüchtigte Femme fatale aus der Feder des dekadenten Romanschriftstellers Pierre Louÿs. / Dans le rôle de Concha, terrible femme fatale imaginée par le romancier décadent Pierre Louÿs.

STILL FROM 'THE DEVIL IS A WOMAN' (1935)
Concha with her young virile lover Antonio (Cesar
Romero). / Concha mit ihrem sehr maskulinen jungen
Liebhaber Antonio (Cesar Romero). / Concha avec son
jeune et viril amant, Antonio (Cesar Romero).

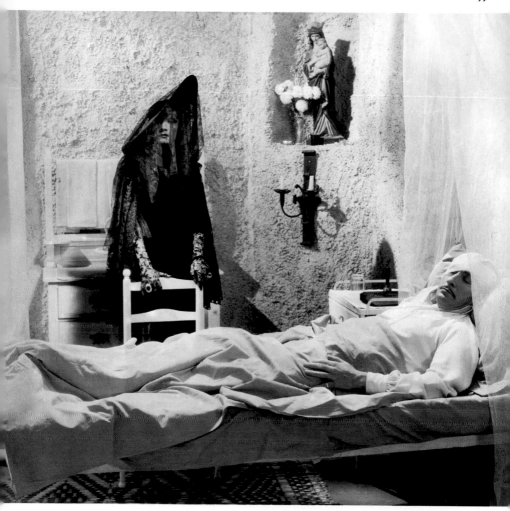

STILL FROM 'THE DEVIL IS A WOMAN' (1935)
With her older slave/lover "Pasqualito" (Lionel Atwill),
looking eerily like von Sternberg himself. / Mit ihrem
älteren Sklaven und Liebhaber „Pasqualito" (Lionel
Atwill), der Sternberg auf unheimliche Weise ähnelt. /
En compagnie de son amant et esclave « Pasqualito »
(Lionel Atwill), qui ressemble étrangement à von
Sternberg.

"*I am Miss Dietrich. Miss Dietrich is me.*"
Josef von Sternberg, director

„*Ich bin Fräulein Dietrich. Fräulein Dietrich ist ich.*"
Josef von Sternberg, Regisseur

«*Je suis Mademoiselle Dietrich. Mademoiselle Dietrich, c'est moi.*»
Josef von Sternberg, cinéaste

**PORTRAIT FOR 'THE DEVIL IS A WOMAN'
(1935)**
Although the mercurial Concha returns to Pasqualito in the movie, in real life Dietrich and von Sternberg separate. / Obwohl die lebhafte Concha im Film zu „Pasqualito" zurückkehrt, gingen Dietrich und Sternberg privat von nun an getrennte Wege. / Bien que l'inconstante Concha revienne vers Pasqualito dans le film, Dietrich et von Sternberg se séparent dans la vraie vie.

PAGE 102
PORTRAIT (1930)

HOLLYWOOD

HOLLYWOOD

HOLLYWOOD

STILL FROM 'I LOVED A SOLDIER' (1936)
A remake of the silent film 'Hotel Imperial,' the film, co-starring Charles Boyer, was never completed. / Dieses Remake des Stummfilms *Hotel Imperial* (1927), diesmal mit Charles Boyer in der männlichen Hauptrolle, wurde nie fertiggestellt. / Remake du film muet *Hotel Imperial*, ce duo avec Charles Boyer restera inachevé.

STILL FROM 'I LOVED A SOLDIER' (1936)
Dietrich and director Henry Hathaway argued over how glamorous she should appear. / Dietrich und der Regisseur Henry Hathaway waren sich uneinig darüber, wie glamourös sie in dieser Rolle erscheinen sollte. / L'actrice et le réalisateur Henry Hathaway sont en désaccord quant au degré de sophistication du personnage.

STILL FROM 'DESIRE' (1936)
Dietrich as jewel thief Madeleine de Beaupré accepts
the homage of her partner in crime (John Halliday). /
In der Rolle der Juwelendiebin Madeleine de Beaupré
nimmt Dietrich die Huldigung ihres Komplizen (John
Halliday) entgegen. / La voleuse de bijoux Madeleine
de Beaupré accepte l'hommage de son complice
(John Halliday).

ON THE SET OF 'DESIRE' (1936)
Using what she learned about lighting and design from
von Sternberg, Dietrich was always demanding about
her look. / Weil sie von Sternberg gelernt hatte, wie
man Ausstattung und Beleuchtung vorteilhaft einsetzt,
stellte Dietrich stets hohe Ansprüche an ihr
Erscheinungsbild. / Forte de la maîtrise des éclairages
et des décors que lui a transmise von Sternberg,
Dietrich se montre toujours très exigeante.

LOBBY CARD FOR 'DESIRE' (1936)

"I never enjoyed working in a film."
Marlene Dietrich

„Die Arbeit beim Film war für mich nie ein Vergnügen."
Marlene Dietrich

« Je n'ai jamais aimé tourner un film. »
Marlene Dietrich

PORTRAIT FOR 'DESIRE' (1936)
Reunited with Gary Cooper who plays automotive engineer Tom Bradley. / Wieder mit Gary Cooper vereint, der den Kraftfahrzeugtechniker Tom Bradley mimt. / Dietrich retrouve Gary Cooper, qui incarne l'ingénieur Tom Bradley.

When their lips meet..

....in the silenc
you'll hear...
a box-office recor
crashing

THEY LOVED EACH OTHER WITH
THE FIERCENESS OF THOSE
WHO HAVE BEEN DENIED LOVE!

Nothing else mattered. As they faced each other, time
stopped in its flight...The memory of barren, bitter years fell
away...nothing remained except the tropic stars, the silent
desert night and the tumultuous beat of their singing hearts!

Selznick International Presents

Marlene DIETRICH
CHARLES BOYER

THE GARDEN OF ALLAH
IN TECHNICOLOR
Produced by DAVID O. SELZNICK
From the book by ROBERT HICHENS • Directed by RICHARD BOLESLAWSKI • Released thru UNITED ARTISTS

ADVERT FOR 'THE GARDEN OF ALLAH' (1936)

ADVERT FOR 'THE GARDEN OF ALLAH' (1936)

"Glamour is what I sell, it's my stock in trade."
Marlene Dietrich

„Glamour ist das, was ich verkaufe, es ist meine Handelsware."
Marlene Dietrich

« Le glamour, c'est mon fonds de commerce. »
Marlene Dietrich

PORTRAIT FOR 'THE GARDEN OF ALLAH' (1936)

Dietrich's publicity photos raise studio promotion to the level of art photography. / Mit den Werbeaufnahmen der Dietrich wird selbst Filmreklame zur Kunst. / Avec Marlene Dietrich, la photo promotionnelle acquiert une dimension artistique.

LOBBY CARD FOR 'KNIGHT WITHOUT ARMOUR' (1937)

STILL FROM 'KNIGHT WITHOUT ARMOUR' (1937)
A big-budget Russian Revolutionary epic, produced by Alexander Korda. / Bei diesem Epos über die Russische Revolution konnte Produzent Alexander Korda aus dem Vollen schöpfen. / Un film épique à gros budget sur la révolution russe, produit par Alexander Korda.

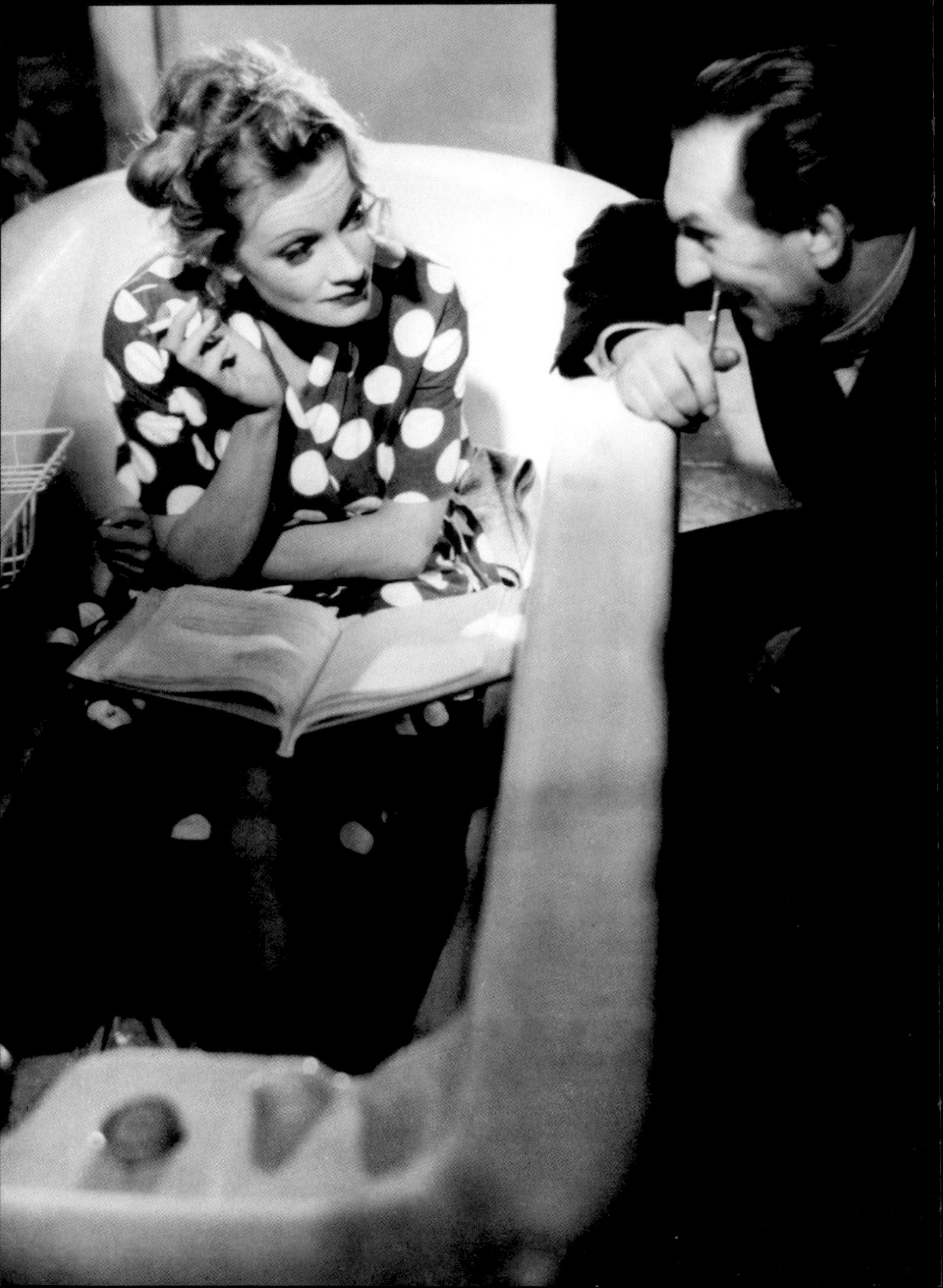

**STILL FROM 'KNIGHT WITHOUT ARMOUR'
(1937)**
Dietrich was always comfortable with her own
sensuality. / Dietrich fühlte sich mit ihrer eigenen
Sinnlichkeit stets wohl. / Dietrich affiche sans
complexes sa propre sensualité.

**ON THE SET OF 'KNIGHT WITHOUT
ARMOUR' (1937)**
Dietrich as Countess Alexandra confers with prestigious
French director Jacques Feyder. / Dietrich, die Gräfin
Alexandra spielt, berät sich hier mit dem renommierten
französischen Regisseur Jacques Feyder. / Dietrich, en
comtesse Alexandra, discute avec le prestigieux
cinéaste français Jacques Feyder.

ON THE SET OF 'ANGEL' (1937)
Fellow German immigrant producer-director Ernst
Lubitsch shares a moment of joy with Dietrich on the
set. / Produzent und Regisseur Ernst Lubitsch, der wie
Dietrich aus Deutschland ausgewandert war, in einem
herzlichen Augenblick während der Dreharbeiten. /
Moment d'hilarité sur le plateau avec le producteur et
réalisateur Ernst Lubitsch, lui aussi d'origine allemande.

PORTRAIT FOR 'ANGEL' (1937)
The way Dietrich liked it, worshiped by two men at the
same time (Herbert Marshall and Melvyn Douglas). /
So gefiel es der Dietrich: von zwei Männern (Herbert
Marshall und Melvyn Douglas) zur gleichen Zeit
umgarnt. / Dietrich dans son rôle favori, celui d'une
femme adulée par deux hommes à la fois (Herbert
Marshall et Melvyn Douglas).

PAGES 120/121
STILL FROM 'DESTRY RIDES AGAIN' (1939)
Dietrich as feisty Frenchy seizes the sacred Western
phallic symbol herself and men hide. / Wenn Dietrich
in der Rolle der streitlustigen Frenchy das heilige
Phallussymbol des „Wilden Westens" selbst in die Hand
nimmt, gehen die Männer in Deckung. / Dans le rôle de
la pétulante Frenchy, Dietrich brandit le symbole
phallique sacré aux yeux des hommes de l'Ouest.

STILL FROM 'DESTRY RIDES AGAIN' (1939)
Dietrich lets her rambunctious, comic side go in this
film. Her opponent is the mild and awkward Jimmy
Stewart as Destry. / In diesem Film lässt Dietrich ihrer
ausgelassenen und komischen Seite freien Lauf. Ihr
Gegenspieler ist der sanftmütige und unbeholfene
Destry, gespielt von Jimmy Stewart. / Face à l'inoffensif
James Stewart dans le rôle de Destry, l'actrice donne
libre cours à son côté comique et exubérant.

*"Her beauty has warmth behind it, and heart, and
she's got the kind of sex appeal that comes across
the screen at you like a ten-ton truck."*
James Stewart

*„Hinter ihrer Schönheit stecken Wärme und Herz,
und sie besitzt die Art von Sex-Appeal, die einen
von der Leinwand her wie ein Zehntonner
überrollt."*
James Stewart

*« Derrière sa beauté, il y a de la chaleur et du
cœur, et elle possède le genre de sex-appeal qui
vous fonce dessus à travers l'écran comme un semi-
remorque. »*
James Stewart

STILL FROM 'DESTRY RIDES AGAIN' (1939)
Dietrich gives the males in the audience what they
want, a 'catfight,' and revitalizes her career. / Dietrich
gibt den männlichen Zuschauern, was sie sich
wünschen: Zickenterror. Ihre Karriere erlebte daraufhin
einen Aufschwung. / Dietrich donne un nouvel élan
à sa carrière en offrant au public masculin un de ces
« crêpages de chignons » dont il est si friand.

PIC

DEC. 10, '40

COVERING THE ENTIRE FIELD OF ENTERTAINMENT

THE FIFTH COLUMN ENTERTAINS

BY U. S. SENATOR
STYLES BRIDGES

10¢ 12 CENTS IN CANADA
DEC. 10, 1940

MARLENE DIETRICH
AND JOHN WAYNE IN
TROPICAL SINNERS

ADVERT FOR 'SEVEN SINNERS' (1940)

COVER OF 'PIC' (10 DECEMBER 1940)

STILL FROM 'SEVEN SINNERS' (1940)
Comedy again, as performer Bijou Blanche on saw, with
Mischa Auer on violin. / Wieder eine Komödie – mit
Bijou Blanche (Dietrich) an der Säge und Sasha
Mencken (Mischa Auer) an der Geige. / Autre comédie
où elle incarne Bijou Blanche, à la scie musicale, avec
Mischa Auer au violon.

STILL FROM 'SEVEN SINNERS' (1940)
Bijou battles jealous tough guy "Little Ned" (Broderick
Crawford). / Bijou prügelt sich mit dem eifersüchtigen
Schurken „Little Ned" (Broderick Crawford). / Bijou en
vient aux mains avec son compagnon jaloux, « Little
Ned » (Broderick Crawford).

**STILL FROM 'THE FLAME OF NEW ORLEANS'
(1941)**
French director René Clair brings his light touch to
the story. The Countess seduces macho ship captain
Bruce Cabot. / Der französische Regisseur Rene Clair
lockert die Geschichte ein wenig auf. Die Gräfin
verführt den machohaften Schiffskapitän (Bruce
Cabot). / La comtesse séduit le capitaine (Bruce Cabot)
sous la direction du cinéaste français René Clair, qui
apporte sa touche de légèreté à l'histoire.

**STILL FROM 'THE FLAME OF NEW ORLEANS'
(1941)**
Dietrich returns to the glamor mode as the
adventuress Countess Ledoux. / Dietrich kehrt mit
der Abenteurerin Gräfin Ledoux wieder zu den
Glamourrollen zurück. / Retour à l'élégance dans le rôle
de l'aventureuse comtesse Ledoux.

130

"Once a woman has forgiven her man, she must not reheat his sins for breakfast."
Marlene Dietrich

„Wenn eine Frau einem Mann einmal vergeben hat, dann muss sie seine Sünden nicht zum Frühstück wieder aufwärmen."
Marlene Dietrich

« Lorsqu'une femme a pardonné à son homme, elle ne doit pas lui resservir ses fautes au petit déjeuner. »
Marlene Dietrich

STILL FROM 'MANPOWER' (1941)
Always dominating the frame, Dietrich in black leather with lover George Raft. / Im Mittelpunkt jeder Einstellung: Fay (Dietrich) in schwarzem Leder mit ihrem Liebhaber (George Raft). / Dominant toujours la scène, Dietrich apparaît en cuir noir auprès de son amant (George Raft).

ON THE SET OF 'THE LADY IS WILLING' (1942)
Director Mitchell Leisen making some final
arrangements before the camera rolls. / Regisseur
Mitchell Leisen legt letzte Hand an, bevor die Kamera
läuft. / Le réalisateur Mitchell Leisen règle les derniers
détails avant de dire « Moteur ! ».

STILL FROM 'THE LADY IS WILLING' (1942)
Five men are better than two when it comes to adoration. / Fünf Verehrer sind besser als zwei. / Cinq hommes valent mieux que deux pour se faire aduler.

"She's not a good actress... but she's always acting. She hardly knows herself anymore."
Fritz Lang, director

„Sie ist keine gute Schauspielerin ... aber sie schauspielert ständig. Sie kennt sich kaum noch selbst."
Fritz Lang, Regisseur

« Ce n'est pas une bonne actrice ... mais elle joue constamment un rôle. Elle ne sait même plus qui elle est. »
Fritz Lang, cinéaste

ALL THE NEW HIT PICTURES IN STORY FORM

MOVIE STORY

MAGAZINE

MOVIE STORY
10¢

MAY

"NO ONE
MAN CAN
THRILL ME"

MARLENE DIETRICH
JOHN WAYNE IN
THE SPOILERS

STILL FROM 'THE SPOILERS' (1942)
Dietrich defends her lover John Wayne, who is
threatened by villainous commissioner Randolph
Scott. / Cherry (Dietrich) verteidigt ihren Liebhaber
(John Wayne), der von einem korrupten Beamten
(Randolph Scott) bedroht wird. / L'héroïne défend son
amant (John Wayne), menacé par un commissaire
véreux (Randolph Scott).

COVER OF 'MOVIE STORY MAGAZINE'
(MAY 1942)

ON THE SET OF 'THE SPOILERS' (1942)
Only a child, Gary Crosby, could get away with holding a gun on Dietrich. / Nur als Kind konnte es sich Gary Crosby leisten, Dietrich mit der Pistole zu bedrohen. / Seul un enfant (Gary Crosby) peut se permettre de menacer Dietrich sans crainte de représailles.

ON THE SET OF 'THE SPOILERS' (1942)
Marked by her sense of humor and love of life, Dietrich joyfully rides a bike in costume. / Mit ihrem typischen Sinn für Humor und ihrer Freude am Leben schwingt sich Dietrich auch im Kostüm aufs Fahrrad. / Donnant libre cours à sa joie de vivre, Marlene Dietrich enfourche une bicyclette en costume de scène.

STILL FROM 'PITTSBURGH' (1942)
Willing to get down and dirty with the guys in real life and in film, with Randolph Scott as Cash Evans. / Im Leben wie im Film ist sie bereit, mit den Kerlen durch dick und dünn zu gehen – hier mit Randolph Scott als Cash Evans. / Prête à mettre les mains dans le cambouis à la ville comme à l'écran, ici avec Randolph Scott dans le rôle de Cash Evans.

PAGES 140/141
ON THE SET OF 'KISMET' (1944)
Reunited with German director William Dieterle, Dietrich plays Jamila in this expressionistic fantasy. / Dieses expressionistische Phantasiestück, in dem sie die Rolle der Jamila spielt, bringt Dietrich wieder mit dem deutschen Regisseur William Dieterle zusammen. / Retrouvailles avec le cinéaste allemand William Dieterle dans une fantaisie expressionniste où elle incarne Jamila.

PORTRAIT FOR 'PITTSBURGH' (1942)
Surrounded by gruff roustabouts, Dietrich dons her more androgynous look. / In dieser Gruppe rauhbeiniger Gelegenheitsarbeiter kleidet sich Dietrich wieder eher androgyn. / Entourée de gaillards bourrus, l'actrice arbore un look plus androgyne.

"Marlene was absolutely sex-ridden but of the theory of sex. She understood sex was the ruling physical thing in human life, but I don't think she was personally a very sexy dame. Sex may have been the guiding force in her life, but intellectually."
Samuel A. Taylor, writer

„Marlene war absolut sexbesessen, aber von der Theorie der Sexualität. Sie erkannte, dass Sex die beherrschende körperliche Angelegenheit im Leben eines Menschen ist, aber ich glaube nicht, dass sie persönlich ein sehr erotisches Weibsbild war. Sex war vielleicht die treibende Kraft in ihrem Leben, aber intellektuell."
Samuel A. Taylor, Autor

« Marlene était absolument obsédée par le sexe, mais du point de vue théorique. Elle savait que la vie humaine était gouvernée par le sexe, mais je ne crois pas qu'elle était personnellement très portée sur la chose. Si le sexe a été le moteur de son existence, c'est sur un plan intellectuel. »
Samuel A. Taylor, auteur

STILL FROM 'KISMET' (1944)
Legendary leg forward, Jamila dances for a drooling Grand Vizier (Edward Arnold). / In legendärer Pose präsentiert sich Jamila tanzend einem geifernden Großwesir (Edward Arnold). / Exhibant ses célèbres jambes, Jamila danse pour un Grand vizir éperdu d'admiration (Edward Arnold).

PAGE 144
BELGIUM (14 FEBRUARY 1945)
During a grueling tour entertaining the troops in North Africa and Europe, Dietrich pauses to wash in Belgium. / Während einer strapaziösen Tournee zur Unterhaltung der amerikanischen Truppen in Nordafrika und Europa erfrischt sich Dietrich in Belgien. / Toilette rafraîchissante en Belgique durant l'éprouvante tournée des troupes postées en Europe et en Afrique du Nord.

GYPSY

ZIGEUNERIN

LA BOHÊME

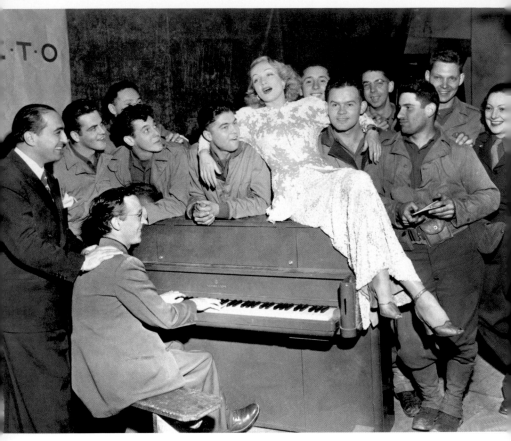

BELGIUM (1944)
Over forty years old, Dietrich still works her magic for the young soldiers on the front. / Obwohl sie bereits die vierzig überschritten hat, betört Dietrich noch immer die jungen Frontsoldaten. / À plus de quarante ans, Dietrich parvient toujours à envoûter les jeunes soldats.

"The German-born Dietrich has spent so many years among the film Jews of Hollywood that her frequent contacts with Jews render her wholly un-German."
Nazi journal 'Der Stürmer'

„Die deutschstämmige Dietrich verbrachte so viele Jahre unter den Filmjuden von Hollywood, dass sie durch ihre häufigen Kontakte mit Juden völlig undeutsch wurde."
NS-Zeitung Der Stürmer

« Bien que née en Allemagne, Dietrich a passé tant d'années au milieu des juifs de Hollywood que ses fréquents contacts avec ces gens l'ont totalement dépouillée de son caractère allemand. »
Journal nazi Der Stürmer

BELGIUM (23 NOVEMBER 1944)
Always fond of gender bending and young men, Dietrich
judges a chorus line of fetching G. I.'s. / Dietrich, die
stets eine Vorliebe für vertauschte Geschlechterrollen
und junge Männer hatte, spielt bei einer Revue
attraktiver G. I.s die Jurorin. / Fidèle à son penchant
pour les jeunes gens et pour l'inversion des rôles,
Dietrich passe en revue une rangée de G. I.

NEW YORK (11 AUGUST 1945)
August 11, 1945: Dietrich welcomes home 14,766
returning soldiers on the Queen Elizabeth / 11. August
1945: Dietrich heißt 14.766 heimkehrende Soldaten an
Bord der Queen Elizabeth willkommen. / Le 11 août 1945,
Marlene Dietrich accueille 14 766 soldats regagnant
l'Amérique à bord du Queen Elizabeth.

BELGIUM (1944)
With composer Irving Berlin at the front. / Mit
Komponist Irving Berlin an der Front. / Sur le front en
compagnie du compositeur Irving Berlin.

STILL FROM 'FOLLOW THE BOYS' (1944)
With friend and political compatriot Orson Welles in a
magic act for the wartime morale booster. / Mit ihrem
guten Freund Orson Welles, der ihr politisch gleich
gesinnt war, bei einer Zaubernummer in diesem Film,
der während des Krieges die Moral stärken sollte. /
Avec son ami et compagnon de combat Orson Welles,
dans un numéro de magie destiné à remonter le moral
de la nation.

STILL FROM 'FOLLOW THE BOYS' (1944)
The "reveal" of the act. / Der große Höhepunkt der
Nummer. / Le clou du numéro.

STILL FROM 'MARTIN ROUMAGNAC' (1946)
Jean Gabin begged "La Grande," as many were calling
Dietrich in Europe, to do this film. / Jean Gabin flehte
„La Grande", wie die Dietrich in Europa von vielen
genannt wurde, an, in diesem Film mitzuspielen. /
« La Grande », comme beaucoup la surnomment en
Europe, accepte de faire ce film sous les supplications
de Jean Gabin.

*"The average man is more interested in a woman
who is interested in him than he is in a woman with
beautiful legs."*
Marlene Dietrich

*„Der Durchschnittsmann ist mehr an einer Frau
interessiert, die sich für ihn interessiert, als an
einer Frau mit langen Beinen."*
Marlene Dietrich

*« L'homme moyen s'intéresse plus à une femme qui
s'intéresse à lui qu'à une femme qui a des jambes
magnifiques. »*
Marlene Dietrich

PORTRAIT FOR 'MARTIN ROUMAGNAC' (1946)
The film was a failure. / Der Film war ein riesiger
Reinfall. / Ce film sera hélas un échec.

STILL FROM 'GOLDEN EARRINGS' (1947)
In the dominant position, the one she most favored,
Dietrich puts blackface on British intelligence officer
Ray Milland. / In der von ihr bevorzugten dominanten
Position schminkt Dietrich den britischen
Geheimdienstler (Ray Milland) schwarz. / Dans la
position dominante qui lui est chère, Dietrich maquille
en noir un officier du renseignement anglais (Ray
Milland).

PORTRAIT FOR 'GOLDEN EARRINGS' (1947)
Director Mitchell Leisen brings back the light touch,
casting Dietrich as the sultry gypsy Lydia. / Mit
Regisseur Mitchell Leisen, der mit ihr die Rolle der
heißblütigen Zigeunerin Lydia besetzt, kehrt sie wieder
zu leichteren Stoffen zurück. / Le réalisateur Mitchell
Leisen ramène un peu de fantaisie en confiant à
Dietrich un rôle de bohémienne sensuelle.

ON THE SET OF 'A FOREIGN AFFAIR' (1948)
Director Billy Wilder shows John Lund how to kiss a
diva. / Regisseur Billy Wilder zeigt John Lund, wie man
eine Diva küsst. / Le cinéaste Billy Wilder montre à
John Lund comment embrasser une diva.

ON THE SET OF 'A FOREIGN AFFAIR' (1948)
Never afraid to flaunt her bisexuality, even in fun,
Dietrich kisses Hedy Lamarr as a prurient Billy Wilder
watches. / Dietrich scheute sich auch im Scherz nie, ihre
Bisexualität zur Schau zu tragen – wie etwa hier, wo sie
unter Billy Wilders lüsternen Blicken Hedy Lamarr
küsst. / Toujours prête à afficher sa bisexualité, Dietrich
embrasse Hedy Lamarr sous le regard émoustillé de
Billy Wilder.

STILL FROM 'A FOREIGN AFFAIR' (1948)
In one of her best films of the Forties, Dietrich
epitomizes the decadence and daring of the long-dead
Weimar era. / In einem ihrer besten Filme aus den
vierziger Jahren verkörpert Dietrich noch einmal die
Dekadenz und Verwegenheit der längst vergangenen
Weimarer Zeit. / Dans l'un de ses meilleurs films des
années quarante, Dietrich incarne la décadence et
l'audace de l'époque de Weimar, depuis longtemps
révolue.

ON THE SET OF 'A FOREIGN AFFAIR' (1948)
Singing to the men, as Wilder looks on. / Sie singt für die
Männer, und Wilder schaut zu. / Dans un numéro de
chant, sous l'œil vigilant de Billy Wilder.

STILL FROM 'JIGSAW' (1949)
Dietrich makes a cameo appearance as a nightclub patron. / Dietrich bei einem Cameo-Auftritt als Gast in einem Nachtklub. / Brève apparition en cliente d'un night-club.

ON THE SET OF 'STAGE FRIGHT' (1950)
Alfred Hitchcock directs a serious Dietrich in the role of the femme fatale Charlotte Inwood. / Alfred Hitchcock gibt einer ernsthaften Dietrich in der Rolle der *Femme fatale* Charlotte Inwood Regieanweisungen. / Attentive aux indications d'Alfred Hitchcock dans le rôle de la femme fatale Charlotte Inwood.

STILL FROM 'NO HIGHWAY IN THE SKY' (1951)
A somewhat distracted engineer played by Jimmy
Stewart finds the glamorous Monica Teasdale (Dietrich)
asleep on his shoulder. / Die traumhafte Monica
Teasdale (Dietrich) ist auf der Schulter eines leicht
zerstreuten Ingenieurs, gespielt von Jimmy Stewart,
eingeschlafen. / Un ingénieur légèrement dérouté
(James Stewart) trouve l'élégante Monica Teasdale
(Dietrich) endormie sur son épaule.

PORTRAIT FOR 'RANCHO NOTORIOUS' (1952)
Although Dietrich battled director Fritz Lang over how
she was photographed, the performance was one of her
best. / Obwohl Dietrich lange mit Regisseur Fritz Lang
diskutierte, wie er sie ins rechte Bild rücken solle, zählte
diese Rolle zu ihren besten. / Bien que la star reproche
à Fritz Lang la manière dont il la filme, elle donne ici
l'une de ses meilleures interprétations.

STILL FROM 'MONTECARLO' (1956)
Dietrich's relationship with co-star (and secret
director) Vittorio de Sica was cold and hostile. /
Dietrichs Verhältnis zu ihrem Schauspielerkollegen
(und heimlichen Regisseur des Films) Vittorio de
Sica war kühl und feindselig. / Une hostilité glacée
règne entre l'actrice et son partenaire Vittorio de
Sica, réalisateur officieux du film.

PORTRAIT FOR 'MONTECARLO' (1956)

STILL FROM 'AROUND THE WORLD IN EIGHTY DAYS' (1956)
Taking time from her busy live performance schedule Dietrich reprised her saloon hostess persona in a small part for producer Mike Todd. / Dietrich nahm sich inmitten ihrer zahlreichen Live-Shows Zeit für einen kurzen Gastauftritt als Animierdame in diesem Film des Produzenten Mike Todd. / Malgré son calendrier de concerts très chargé, Marlene Dietrich retrouve son personnage d'entraîneuse de saloon pour un petit rôle dans ce film produit par Mike Todd.

ON THE SET OF 'AROUND THE WORLD IN EIGHTY DAYS' (1956)
Now into her fifties, Dietrich still exhibits her much valorized legs. / Auch nachdem sie die fünfzig überschritten hat, zeigt Dietrich noch immer ihre unschätzbar wertvollen Beine. / La cinquantaine bien entamée, Dietrich continue à exhiber ses jambes.

**STILL FROM 'WITNESS FOR THE
PROSECUTION' (1957)**
Dietrich as the ex-cabaret singer Christine Helm, based
on her character in 'A Foreign Affair,' with Tyrone Power
as her husband. / Dietrich als ehemalige Varietésängerin
Christine Helm, ähnlich ihrer Rolle in *Eine auswärtige
Affäre*, mit Tyrone Power als ihrem Ehemann. / Dans le
rôle de l'ancienne chanteuse de cabaret Christine Helm,
inspirée de son personnage dans *La Scandaleuse de
Berlin*, avec Tyrone Power pour époux.

**PORTRAIT FOR 'WITNESS FOR THE
PROSECUTION' (1957)**

MAKE-UP TEST FOR 'WITNESS FOR THE PROSECUTION' (1957)
Dietrich's double role as a Cockney woman is praised by the few critics who recognized her. This make-up was vetoed. / Dietrichs Doppelrolle mit Cockney-Akzent wurde von den wenigen Kritikern, die sie erkannt hatten, gelobt. Gegen diese Maske legte sie Einspruch ein. / Essai de maquillage (non retenu) pour son deuxième rôle dans le film, salué par les rares critiques qui reconnaissent la star sous les traits d'une femme du peuple.

ON THE SET OF 'WITNESS FOR THE PROSECUTION' (1957)
Proof sheets of Dietrich rehearsing with Wilder and co-star Charles Laughton, who coached her on her accent. / Diese Abzüge zeigen Dietrich bei der Probe mit Wilder und ihrem Kollegen Charles Laughton, der ihr half, den Cockney-Akzent zu erlernen. / Épreuves des répétitions avec Billy Wilder et son partenaire Charles Laughton, qui lui apprend à parler avec l'accent populaire de son personnage.

WP-106-1

WP-106-5

WP-106-9

-2

-6

-10

-3

-7

-11

8

-12

STILL FROM 'TOUCH OF EVIL' (1958)
Friend Orson Welles, playing corrupt cop Hank Quinlan,
casts Dietrich as the gypsy Tanya in his classy noir film. /
Ihr Freund Orson Welles, der den korrupten Polizisten
Hank Quinlan spielt, gab Dietrich die Rolle der
Zigeunerin Tanya in seinem klassischen *Film noir*. / Son
ami Orson Welles, qui interprète le policier corrompu
Hank Quinlan, lui confie un rôle de bohémienne dans ce
classique du film noir.

STILL FROM 'JUDGMENT AT NUREMBERG'
(1961)
Director Stanley Kramer humbly credited Dietrich with
being the "heart and soul" of the film, here playing
opposite Spencer Tracy. / Bescheiden bezeichnete
Regisseur Stanley Kramer Dietrich – hier an der Seite
von Spencer Tracy – als „Herz und Seele" des Films. /
Dietrich, ici aux côtés de Spencer Tracy, est
humblement considérée comme « l'âme du film » par
le réalisateur Stanley Kramer.

"The weak are more likely to make the strong weak
than the strong are likely to make the weak
strong."
Marlene Dietrich

„Es ist wahrscheinlicher, dass die Schwachen die
Starken schwächen als dass die Starken die
Schwachen stärken."
Marlene Dietrich

« Les faibles ont plus de chances d'affaiblir les forts
que les forts n'en ont de renforcer les faibles. »
Marlene Dietrich

STILL FROM 'PARIS, WHEN IT SIZZLES' (1964)
Director Richard Quine uses Dietrich's iconic status in a
cameo for his film. / Regisseur Richard Quine nutzt den
Status der Dietrich als Ikone für einen Cameo-Auftritt
in seinem Film. / Le réalisateur Richard Quine exploite
le statut mythique de Dietrich pour cette brève
apparition dans son film.

"I am not a myth."
Marlene Dietrich

„Ich bin kein Mythos."
Marlene Dietrich

« Je ne suis pas un mythe. »
Marlene Dietrich

ON THE SET OF 'JUST A GIGOLO' (1979)
After 'Judgment at Nuremberg,' Dietrich did not appear
in a major role until 1979. She is with director and co-star
David Hemmings. / Nach *Das Urteil von Nürnberg*
spielte Dietrich bis 1979 keine größeren Rollen mehr.
Hier ist sie mit dem Regisseur und Schauspielerkollegen
David Hemmings zu sehen. / Après *Jugement à
Nuremberg*, Marlene Dietrich ne joue plus de grands
rôles jusqu'en 1979. Elle est ici aux côtés de son
partenaire et metteur en scène David Hemmings.

SAHARA HOTEL, LAS VEGAS (13 MAY 1959)
Dietrich does a high kick at the end of her show at the Sahara Hotel in Las Vegas. / Dietrich schwingt das Bein am Ende ihrer Show im Sahara-Hotel von Las Vegas. / Partie de «jambes en l'air» à la fin de son spectacle au Sahara Hotel de Las Vegas.

PAGE 178
**COVER OF 'MOTION PICTURE'
(DECEMBER 1931)**

PORTRAIT (1955)
Dietrich expanded and improved her popular live stage shows until the last one in 1975. / Dietrich erweiterte und verbesserte ihre beliebte Bühnenshow bis zu ihrem letzten Auftritt im Jahre 1975. / Marlene Dietrich continue d'améliorer son spectacle jusqu'à la toute dernière représentation, en 1975.

Motion Picture

December **25 cents**

MARLENE DIETRI

The
"MOVIE HEROES"
of the
World War

HOW HOLLYWOOD
GETS ITS
WILD REPUTATION

3
CHRONOLOGY

CHRONOLOGIE

CHRONOLOGIE

CHRONOLOGY

27 December 1901 Birth of Marie Magdalene Dietrich in Berlin.

1908 Father, Louis Erich Otto Dietrich, dies of syphilis.

1921 Begins working in cabarets.

1922 First acting jobs in Berlin theaters, including with Max Reinhardt. Begins movie career; becomes infamous for her gender-bending roles.

1923 Marries theater director Rudolf Sieber.

1924 Daughter Maria born.

1927 Cast in her first lead role in *Café Elektric*.

1929 Cast by Josef von Sternberg in *The Blue Angel*, beginning her tempestuous and sadomasochistic partnership with the director.

1930 Signed by Paramount and leaves for the United States; makes *Morocco* with von Sternberg; nominated for an Academy Award; brings her daughter to Hollywood but husband remains in Europe.

1932 Makes *Blonde Venus*; sued by von Sternberg's wife for "alienation of affections."

1933 Rejects offer by Nazis to return to Germany and make films.

1934 Stars in *The Scarlet Empress*.

1935 *The Devil Is a Woman*, her last film with von Sternberg, is a thinly veiled overview of their relationship.

1937 Highest-paid female star in Hollywood; takes on American citizenship out of disgust with Nazi Germany.

1939 Reinvents herself in the comic Western *Destry Rides Again*.

1943–1945 Entertains the troops throughout Europe and North Africa and broadcasts into Nazi Germany, singing German songs; also appears in several anti-Nazi propaganda films.

1945 Returns to Germany to bury her mother and see her sister.

1947 Receives the U.S. Medal of Freedom for her work during the war.

1949 Receives the title of 'Chevalier de la Légion d'Honneur.'

1953 Performs one-woman shows in Las Vegas, London, and Paris.

1957 Double role in Billy Wilder's *Witness for the Prosecution*.

1960 Tours Germany with her act.

1961 Appears in the landmark film *Judgment at Nuremberg*.

1965 Diagnosed with cervical cancer, undergoes treatment.

1967 Opens her successful show on Broadway.

1973–1975 Several injuries related to performances, hospitalized, retires from touring.

1978 Makes her last feature film appearance in *Just a Gigolo*.

1979 Autobiography *My Life* is published.

6 May 1992 Dies in Paris.

COVER OF 'SCREEN BOOK' (FEBRUARY 1939)

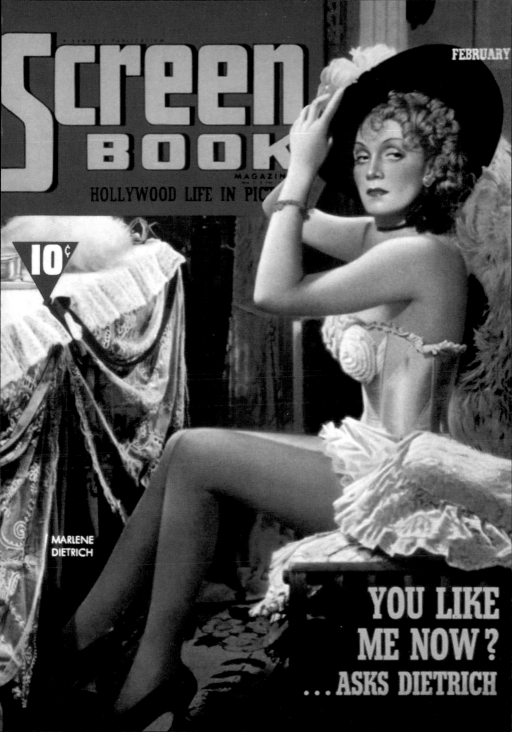

THE

New Movie

MAGAZINE

A TOWER MAGAZINE

MAGAZINE

JUNE
10¢

15¢ in Canada

NRA

MARLENE
DIETRICH

MAE WEST —
Is her influence
GOOD or BAD?

CLARK GABLE
ANSWERS "WHAT IS YOUR POWER OVER WOMEN?"

CHRONOLOGIE

27. Dezember 1901 Sie wird als Marie Magdalene Dietrich in Berlin geboren.

1908 Ihr Vater Louis Erich Otto Dietrich stirbt an Syphilis.

1921 Sie beginnt mit Auftritten im Varieté.

1922 Erste kleinere Schauspielrollen an Berliner Bühnen, unter anderem bei Max Reinhardt. Sie beginnt ihre Filmkarriere und wird berüchtigt für ihre androgynen Rollen.

1923 Sie heiratet den Theaterregisseur Rudolf Sieber.

1924 Ihre Tochter Maria kommt zur Welt.

1927 Sie erhält ihre erste Hauptrolle in dem Film *Café Elektric*.

1929 Mit ihrer Rolle in seinem Film *Der blaue Engel* beginnt zugleich eine stürmische und sadomasochistische Beziehung zu dem Regisseur Josef von Sternberg (bürgerlich: Jonas Sternberg).

1930 Sie wird von Paramount unter Vertrag genommen und wandert in die Vereinigten Staaten aus. Dort dreht sie *Marokko* (aka *Herzen in Flammen*) unter Sternberg und wird für einen Academy Award („Oscar") nominiert. Sie holt ihre Tochter nach Hollywood, während ihr Ehemann in Europa bleibt.

1932 Sie dreht *Blonde Venus* und wird von der Ehefrau von Sternbergs wegen Ehebruchs verklagt.

1933 Sie lehnt ein Angebot der Nationalsozialisten ab, nach Deutschland zurückzukehren und dort Filme zu drehen.

1934 Sie spielt die Titelrolle in *Die scharlachrote Kaiserin* (aka *Zarewna*).

1935 *Der Teufel ist eine Frau* (aka *Die spanische Tänzerin*), ihr letzter Film mit Sternberg, ist eine kaum verschleierte Zusammenfassung ihrer Beziehung zu ihm.

1937 Sie wird zum höchstbezahlten weiblichen Hollywood-Star und nimmt aus Abscheu vor dem nationalsozialistisch regierten Deutschland die US-Staatsbürgerschaft an.

1939 In der Westernkomödie *Destry reitet wieder* (aka *Der große Bluff*) gibt sie sich ein neues Image.

1943–1945 Sie unterhält die Truppen in Europa und Nordafrika und singt deutsche Lieder, die über den Rundfunk nach Deutschland ausgestrahlt werden. Zudem tritt sie in mehreren Propaganda-Filmen auf, die sich gegen das NS-Regime richten.

1945 Sie kehrt zum Begräbnis ihrer Mutter nach Deutschland zurück. Dort trifft sie auch ihre Schwester wieder.

1947 Sie erhält die Freiheitsmedaille („Medal of Freedom") der Vereinigten Staaten für ihre Tätigkeit während des Krieges.

1949 Sie erhält von Frankreich den Titel „Ritter der Ehrenlegion" („chevalier de la Légion d'honneur").

1953 Sie tritt in einer „Ein-Frau-Show" in Las Vegas, London und Paris auf.

1957 Sie spielt eine Doppelrolle in Billy Wilders *Zeugin der Anklage*.

1960 Sie geht mit ihrem Programm auf Tournee durch Deutschland.

1961 Sie tritt in dem bahnbrechenden Film *Das Urteil von Nürnberg* auf.

1965 Nachdem man Gebärmutterhalskrebs bei ihr festgestellt hat, lässt sie sich behandeln.

1967 Sie beginnt eine erfolgreiche Broadway-Show.

1973–1975 Nach mehreren Verletzungen im Rahmen ihrer Auftritte kommt sie ins Krankenhaus und beendet ihre Tourneen.

1978 Sie tritt in *Schöner Gigolo, armer Gigolo* zum letzten Mal in einem Spielfilm auf.

1979 Ihre Autobiographie *Nehmt nur mein Leben* erscheint.

6. Mai 1992 Sie stirbt in Paris.

COVER OF 'NEW MOVIE' (JUNE 1934)

CHRONOLOGIE

27 décembre 1901 Naissance de Marie Magdalene Dietrich à Berlin.

1908 Son père, Louis Erich Otto Dietrich, meurt de la syphilis.

1921 Commence à travailler dans des cabarets.

1922 Décroche ses premiers rôles dans des théâtres berlinois, notamment avec Max Reinhardt. Débute sa carrière cinématographique. Ses rôles androgynes lui valent une réputation sulfureuse.

1923 Épouse l'assistant de production Rudolf Sieber.

1924 Naissance de leur fille Maria.

1927 Obtient le premier rôle dans *Filles d'amour*.

1929 Incarne Lola Lola dans *L'Ange bleu* de Josef von Sternberg. C'est le début d'une relation houleuse et sadomasochiste avec le cinéaste.

1930 Signe un contrat avec la Paramount et part pour les États-Unis ; tourne *Cœurs brûlés* avec von Sternberg ; est sélectionnée pour les Oscars ; fait venir sa fille à Hollywood tandis que son mari reste en Europe.

1932 Tourne *La Vénus blonde* ; est poursuivie par la femme de von Sternberg pour « détournement d'affection ».

1933 Rejette la proposition des nazis de revenir tourner en Allemagne.

1934 Tourne *L'Impératrice rouge*.

1935 *La Femme et le Pantin*, son dernier film avec von Sternberg, est un portrait à peine voilé de leur relation.

1937 Devient l'actrice la mieux payée de Hollywood ; dégoûtée par l'Allemagne nazie, elle acquiert la nationalité américaine.

1939 Se réinvente dans le western comique *Femme ou démon*.

1943-1945 Soutient le moral des troupes à travers l'Europe et l'Afrique du Nord et chante sur les ondes en direction de l'Allemagne ; apparaît également dans plusieurs films de propagande antinazie.

1945 Retourne en Allemagne pour assister à l'enterrement de sa mère et rendre visite à sa sœur.

1947 Reçoit la Médaille de la liberté aux États-Unis pour son action durant la guerre.

1949 Est nommée chevalier de la Légion d'honneur en France.

1953 Monte un tour de chant à Las Vegas, Londres et Paris.

1957 Double rôle dans *Témoin à charge* de Billy Wilder.

1960 Donne son tour de chant en Allemagne.

1961 Apparaît dans le film *Jugement à Nuremberg*.

1965 Atteinte d'un cancer cervical, elle subit un traitement.

1967 Lance un spectacle couronné de succès à Broadway.

1973-1975 Hospitalisée à la suite de plusieurs blessures occasionnées par ses spectacles, elle se retire de la scène.

1978 Dernière apparition au cinéma dans le film *Just a Gigolo*.

1979 Publication de son autobiographie, *My Life* (parue en français en 1984 sous le titre *Marlene D.*).

6 mai 1992 Décède à Paris.

ADVERT FOR 'SHANGHAI EXPRESS' (1932)

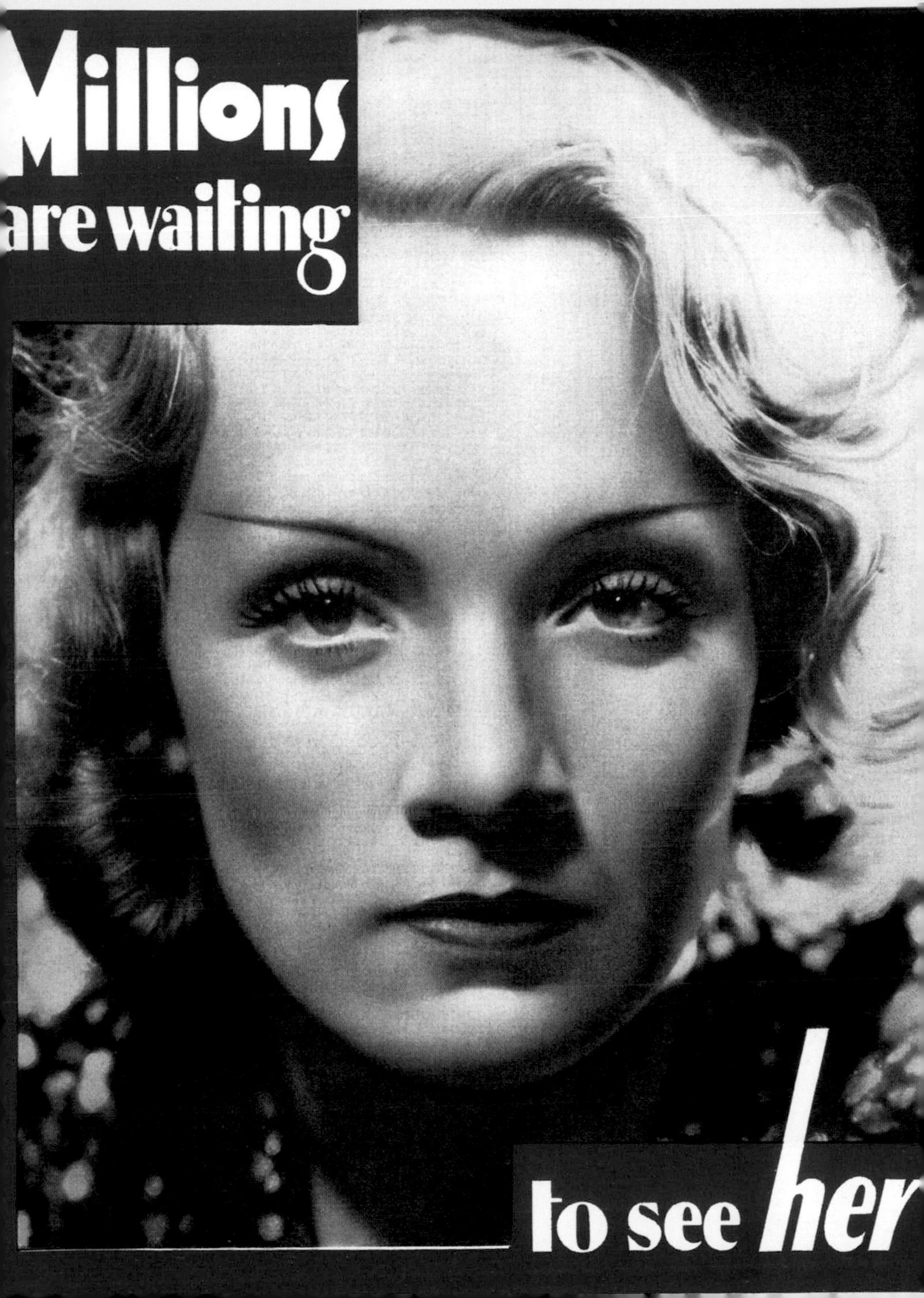
Millions
are waiting
to see her

4
FILMOGRAPHY

FILMOGRAFIE

FILMOGRAPHIE

Der Tänzer meiner Frau (eng. 'My Wife's Dancing Partner', 1925)
Dancer/Tänzerin/danseuse. Director/Regie/réalisation: Alexander Korda.

Der Juxbaron (eng. 'The Bogus Baron', fr. *Le Baron imaginaire*, 1926)
Sophie. Director/Regie/réalisation: Willi Wolff.

Manon Lescaut (dt. aka *Die Geliebte des Abbé*, 1926)
Micheline. Director/Regie/réalisation: Arthur Robison.

Madame wünscht keine Kinder (eng. 'Madame Doesn't Want Children', fr. *Madame ne veut pas d'enfant*, 1926)
Small part/Komparsenrolle/figuration.
Director/Regie/réalisation: Alexander Korda.

Eine Dubarry von heute (eng. 'Madame Dubarry', 1927)
Kokotte/Cocotte. Director/Regie/réalisation: Alexander Korda.

Kopf hoch, Charly! (eng. 'Chin up, Charly', fr. *Tête haute, Charly!*, 1927)
Edmée. Director/Regie/réalisation: Willi Wolff.

Im Schatten des Glücks (1919)
Small part/Komparsenrolle/figuration.
Directors/Regie/réalisation: Jacob & Luis Fleck.

Tragödie der Liebe (eng. 'Tragedy of Love', fr. *La Tragédie de l'amour*, 1923)
Lucy. Director/Regie/réalisation: Joe May.

So sind die Männer (aka *Der Kleine Napoleon* [dt. aka *Napoleons kleiner Bruder*], fr. *Le Petit Napoléon*, 1923)
Kathrin. Director/Regie/réalisation: Georg Jacoby.

Der Mensch am Wege (eng. 'Man by the Wayside', fr. *L'Homme au bord de la route*, 1923)
Grocer's daughter/Krämerstochter/La fille de l'épicier.
Director/Regie/réalisation: William Dieterle.

Der Mönch von Santarem (aka *Der Mönch von Santarem*, 1924)
Small part/Komparsenrolle/figuration.
Director/Regie/réalisation: Lothar Mendes.

Der Sprung ins Leben (dt. aka *Der Roman eines Zirkuskindes*, eng. 'Leap into Life', 1924)
Small part/Komparsenrolle/figuration.
Director/Regie/réalisation: Johannes Guter.

Sein größter Bluff (eng. 'His Biggest Bluff', 1927)
Yvette. Directors/Regie/réalisation: Henrik Galeen & Harry Piel.

Café Elektric (dt. *Prostitution - Irrwege der Liebe* [aka *Prostitution - Das Kaufhaus der Liebe/Wenn ein Weib den Weg verliert/Die Liebesbörse*], fr. *Filles d'amour*, 1927)
Erni. Director/Regie/réalisation: Gustav Ucicky.

Prinzessin Olala (fr. *Princesse Olala*, 1928)
Chichotte. Director/Regie/réalisation: Robert Land.

Die glückliche Mutter (eng. 'The Happy Mother', 1928)
As herself/als sie selbst/dans son propre rôle.
Director/Regie/réalisation: Rudolf Sieber.

Gefahren der Brautzeit (dt. aka *Liebesnächte/Liebesbriefe/Im Banne der Frauen/Aus dem Tagebuch eines Verführers*, eng. 'Dangers of the Engagement Period', 1929)
Evelyne. Director/Regie/réalisation: Fred Sauer.

Ich küsse Ihre Hand, Madame (eng. 'I Kiss Your Hand, Madame', fr. *Je baise votre main, Madame*, 1929)
Laurence. Director/Regie/réalisation: Robert Land.

Die Frau, nach der man sich sehnt (eng. 'The Woman One Longs For', fr. *L'Énigme*, 1929)
Stascha. Director/Regie/réalisation: Curtis Bernhardt.

Das Schiff der verlorenen Menschen (eng. 'The Ship of Lost Souls', fr. *Le Navire des hommes perdus*, 1929)
Ethel. Director/Regie/réalisation: Maurice Tourneur.

Der blaue Engel (eng. 'The Blue Angel', fr. *L'Ange bleu*, 1930)
Lola Lola. Director/Regie/réalisation: Josef von Sternberg.

Morocco (dt. *Marokko* [aka *Herzen in Flammen*], fr. *Cœurs brûlés*, 1930)
Amy Jolly. Director/Regie/réalisation: Josef von Sternberg.

Dishonored (dt. *Entehrt*, fr. *Agent X27*, 1931)
Marie (Kolverer)/X27. Director/Regie/réalisation: Josef von Sternberg.

Shanghai Express (dt. *Shanghai-Express*, 1932)

Shanghai Lily/Magdalen. Director/Regie/réalisation: Josef von Sternberg.

Blonde Venus (fr. *La Vénus blonde*, 1932)
Helen Faraday/Helen Jones. Director/Regie/réalisation: Josef von Sternberg.

The Song of Songs (dt. *Das Hohe Lied*, fr. *Cantique d'amour*, 1933)
Lily. Director/Regie/réalisation: Rouben Mamoulian.

The Scarlet Empress (dt. *Die scharlachrote Kaiserin* [aka *Zarewna*], fr. *L'Impératrice rouge*, 1934)
Catherine II. Director/Regie/réalisation: Josef von Sternberg.

The Fashion Side of Hollywood (1935)
As herself/als sie selbst/dans son propre rôle. Director/Regie/réalisation: Josef von Sternberg.

The Devil Is a Woman (dt. *Der Teufel ist eine Frau* [aka *Die spanische Tänzerin*], fr. *La Femme et le Pantin*, 1935)
Concha. Director/Regie/réalisation: Josef von Sternberg.

I Loved a Soldier (1936)
Anna. Director/Regie/réalisation: Henry Hathaway.

Desire (dt. *Sehnsucht* **[aka** *Perlen zum Glück***],
fr.** *Désir***, 1936)**
Madeleine. Director/Regie/réalisation: Frank Borzage.

The Garden of Allah (dt. *Der Garten Allahs,*
fr. *Le Jardin d'Allah***, 1936)**
Domini. Director/Regie/réalisation: Richard
Boleslawski.

Knight without Armour (dt. *Tatjana*
[aka *Ein schweigsamer Held/Leidenschaft***],
fr.** *Le Chevalier sans armure***, 1937)**
Countess/Gräfin/Comtesse Alexandra.
Director/Regie/réalisation: Jacques Feyder.

Angel (dt. *Engel,* **fr.** *Ange***, 1937)**
Maria/Angel/Mrs. Brown. Director/Regie/réalisation:
Ernst Lubitsch.

Destry Rides Again (dt. *Destry reitet wieder*
[aka *Der große Bluff***], fr.** *Femme ou démon***, 1939)**
Frenchy. Director/Regie/réalisation: George Marshall.

Seven Sinners (dt. *Sieben Sünder* **[aka** *Das Haus
der sieben Sünden***], fr.** *La Maison des sept péchés,*
1940)
Bijou. Director/Regie/réalisation: Tay Garnett.

The Flame of New Orleans (dt. *Die Flamme von
New Orleans* **[aka** *Die Abenteurerin***], fr.** *La Belle
Ensorceleuse***, 1941)**
Countess/Gräfin/Comtesse Claire Ledoux/Lili.
Director/Regie/réalisation: René Clair.

Manpower (dt. *Herzen in Flammen* **[aka** *Gefährliche
Freundschaft***], fr.** *L'Entraîneuse fatale***, 1941)**
Fay. Director/Regie/réalisation: Raoul Walsh.

The Lady Is Willing (dt. *Fräulein Mama* **[aka** *Ich
heirate eine Verrückte***], fr.** *Madame veut un bébé,*
1942)
Elizabeth. Director/Regie/réalisation: Mitchell Leisen.

The Spoilers (dt. *Die Freibeuterin* **[aka** *Stahlharte
Fäuste/Eine Frau ohne Moral/ Goldrausch in
Alaska***], fr.** *Les Écumeurs***, 1942)**
Cherry Malotte. Director/Regie/réalisation: Ray
Enright.

Pittsburgh (1942)
Josie. Director/Regie/réalisation: Lewis Seiler.

Show Business at War (1943)
As herself/als sie selbst/dans son propre rôle.
Director/Regie/réalisation: Louis De Rochemont.

Kismet (1944)
Jamila. Director/Regie/réalisation: William Dieterle.

Follow the Boys (aka 'Hollywood Parade', 1944)
As herself/als sie selbst/dans son propre rôle.
Director/Regie/réalisation: A. Edward Sutherland.

Martin Roumagnac (1946)
Blanche. Director/Regie/réalisation: Georges Lacombe.

Golden Earrings (dt. *Goldene Ohrringe*, fr. *Les Anneaux d'or*, 1947)
Lydia. Director/Regie/réalisation: Mitchell Leisen.

A Foreign Affair (dt. *Eine auswärtige Affäre*, fr. *La Scandaleuse de Berlin*, 1948)
Erika. Director/Regie/réalisation: Billy Wilder.

Jigsaw (fr. *L'Ange de la haine*, 1949)
Cameo/Gast im Nachtklub/brève apparition. Director/Regie/réalisation: Fletcher Markle.

Stage Fright (dt. *Die rote Lola*, fr. *Le Grand Alibi*, 1950)
Charlotte. Director/Regie/réalisation: Alfred Hitchcock.

No Highway in the Sky (dt. *Die Reise ins Ungewisse*, fr. *Le Voyage fantastique*, 1951)
Monica. Director/Regie/réalisation: Henry Koster.

Rancho Notorious (dt. *Engel der Gejagten* [aka *Die Gejagten*], fr. *L'Ange des maudits*, 1952)
Altar Keane. Director/Regie/réalisation: Fritz Lang.

Montecarlo (aka 'The Monte Carlo Story', fr. *Une histoire de Monte Carlo*, 1956)
Maria. Director/Regie/réalisation: Sam Taylor.

Around the World in Eighty Days (dt. *In 80 Tagen um die Welt*, fr. *Le Tour du monde en quatre-vingts jours*, 1956)
Saloon hostess/Freudenmädchen/entraîneuse de saloon. Director/Regie/réalisation: Michael Anderson.

Witness for the Prosecution (dt. *Zeugin der Anklage*, fr. *Témoin à charge*, 1957)
Christine. Director/Regie/réalisation: Billy Wilder.

Touch of Evil (dt. *Im Zeichen des Bösen*, fr. *La Soif du mal*, 1958)
Tanya. Director/Regie/réalisation: Orson Welles.

Judgment at Nuremberg (dt. *Das Urteil von Nürnberg*, fr. *Jugement à Nuremberg*, 1961)
Mrs. Bertholt/Frau Bertholt/Mme Bertholt. Director/Regie/réalisation: Stanley Kramer.

Black Fox: The True Story of Adolf Hitler (1962)
Narrator/Sprecherin/narratrice. Director/Regie/réalisation: Louis Stoumen.

Paris, When It Sizzles (dt. *Zusammen in Paris*, fr. *Deux têtes folles*, 1964)
Cameo/Cameo-Auftritt/brève apparition. Director/Regie/réalisation: Richard Quine.

A Night of Thoughts (dt. *Der gewöhnliche Faschismus*, 1965)
As herself/als sie selbst/dans son propre rôle. Director/Regie/réalisation: Mikhail Romm.

Magic of Marlene (1968)
As herself/als sie selbst/dans son propre rôle. Director/Regie/réalisation: Norman Spencer.

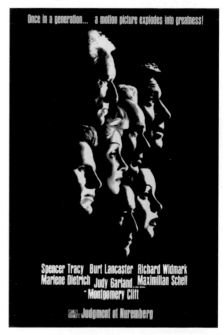

I Wish You Love (1973)
As herself/als sie selbst/dans son propre rôle Director/Regie/réalisation: Clark Jones.

Just a Gigolo (1979)
Baroness von Semering/Baroness von Semering/Baronne von Semering.
Director/Regie/réalisation: David Hemmings.

Marlene (1984)
As herself/als sie selbst/dans son propre rôle. Director/Regie/réalisation: Maximilian Schell.

BIBLIOGRAPHY

Bemmann, Helga: *Marlene Dietrich.* VEB, 1987.
Brooks, Louise: *'Marlene.'* Positif 75, May 1966.
Carr, Larry: *Four Fabulous Faces.* Penguin, 1978.
Dickens, Homer: *The Films of Marlene Dietrich.* Citadel Press, 1968.
Dietrich, Marlene: *My Life.* Weidenfeld and Nicolson, 1989.
Dietrich, Marlene: *Marlene Dietrich's ABC.* Doubleday, 1962.
Dietrich, Marlene: *Marlene D.* Ducout, 1984.
Dietrich, Marlene: *Vogue par Marlene Dietrich.* Condé Nast, 1973.
Dietrich, Marlene: *'How To Be Loved.'* Ladies Home Journal, January 1954.
Frewin, Leslie: *Blonde Venus: A Life of Marlene Dietrich.* Roy, 1955.
Griffith, Richard: *Marlene Dietrich: Image and Legend.* MoMA, 1959.
Hessel, Franz: *Marlene Dietrich.* Kindt and Bucher, 1931.
Higham, Charles: *Marlene: The Life of Marlene Dietrich.* W. W. Norton, 1977.
Knight, Arthur: *'Marlene Dietrich: Notes on a Living Legend.'* Films in Review, December 1954.
Kobal, John: *Marlene Dietrich.* Studio Vista, 1968.
Manfred, Georg: *Marlene Dietrich. Künstler und Filme,* 1931.
Martin, W.K.: *Marlene Dietrich.* Chelsea Publishers, 1994.

Mollica, Vincenzo (ed.): *Marlene Dietrich and Betty Boop.* Editori del Grifo, 1985.
Morley, Sheridan: *Marlene Dietrich.* Sphere Books, 1978.
Noa, Wolfgang: *Marlene Dietrich.* Henschelverlag, 1975.
O'Conner, Patrick: *The Amazing Blonde Women: Dietrich's Own Style.* Bloomsbury, 1991.
Riva, Maria: *Marlene Dietrich.* Knopf, 1993.
Riva, Maria & Naudet, Jean Jacques: *Marlene Dietrich, Photographs and Memories.* Knopf, 2001.
Salmon, André: *Marlene Dietrich.* Nouvelle Libraire Française, 1932
Sarris, Andrew: *The Films of Josef von Sternberg.* MoMA, 1966.
Seydel, Renate: *Marlene Dietrich.* Henschelverlag, 1984.
Skærved, Malene Sheppard: *Dietrich.* Haus Publishing, 2003.
Spoto, Donald: *Dietrich.* Bantam, 1988.
Studlar, Gaylyn: *In the Realm of Pleasure: Von Sternberg, Dietrich, and the Masochistic Ethic.* University of Illinois, 1988.
Sudendorf, Werner: *Marlene Dietrich.* DTV, 2001.
Von Sternberg, Josef: *Fun in a Chinese Laundry.* Macmillan, 1965.
Walker, Alexander: *Dietrich.* Harper and Row, 1984.

IMPRINT

© 2007 TASCHEN GmbH
Hohenzollernring 53, D-50672 Köln
www.taschen.com

Editor/Picture Research/Layout: Paul Duncan/Wordsmith Solutions
Editorial Coordination: Martin Holz, Cologne
Production Coordination: Nadia Najm and Horst Neuzner, Cologne
German Translation: Thomas J. Kinne, Nauheim
French Translation: Anne Le Bot, Paris
Multilingual Production: www.arnaudbriand.com, Paris
Typeface Design: Sense/Net, Andy Disl and Birgit Reber, Cologne

Printed in Italy
ISBN 978-3-8228-2211-1

To stay informed about upcoming TASCHEN titles, please request
our magazine at www.taschen.com/magazine or write to TASCHEN,
Hohenzollernring 53, D-50672 Cologne, Germany,
contact@taschen.com, Fax: +49-221-254919. We will be happy to
send you a free copy of our magazine which is filled with
information about all of our books.